E-MAN

Life in the NYPD
Emergency Service Unit

by
Det. Al Sheppard, Ret.
with
Jerry Schmetterer

IUniverse Star

New York   Bloomington

E-Man
Life in the NYPD Emergency Services Unit

iUniverse Star
an iUniverse, Inc. imprint

iUniverse books may be ordered through booksellers or by contacting:

iUniverse
1663 Liberty Drive
Bloomington, IN 47403
www.iuniverse.com
1-800-Authors (1-800-288-4677)

ISBN: 978-1-935278-26-9 (pbk)
ISBN: 978-1-935278-27-6 (ebk)

Library of Congress Control Number: 2009923042

Printed in the United States of America

iUniverse rev. date: 2/12/2009

"When people need help, they call the police; when the police need help, they call Emergency Services."

Acknowledgments

The authors wish to thank **all** the brave men and women throughout the world whose sacrifices make it possible for us to enjoy freedom and safety in these difficult times.

I would like to also forever acknowledge a number of special people in my life beginning with my late father, Watt Sheppard, who instilled in me many things but especially discipline, integrity, and an appreciation of my roots. He also taught me to fight for the rights of working men and to protect those who were treated unfairly. I wish to mention my mom and stepfather, Virginia and Tom Toscano, for all of their support and understanding. My wonderful wife, Patricia, should also be recognized for her support, caring, and her patience, especially as I battled and overcame many health problems. Of course, there are also my children who I am so proud of: Al Jr., John L., Robert, and the girls Kelly, Christina, and Camille, all of whom are beautiful, talented, and caring. I also would like to mention Dr. William V. Campbell and his wife of fifty-eight years, Miss Dot Marie, two of the kindest and most wonderful people I have ever met. Finally, I pay tribute to my beloved mother, Virginia Sheppard, who will forever remain close to my heart.
—Al Sheppard, April 2006

To Emily for her consistent support for all my "projects" and to Annette for her boundless encouragement.
—Jerry Schmetterer, April 2006

Special Acknowledgments

The authors wish to bring special attention to Sheldon Shuch, PhD, whose help in writing this memoir was invaluable. Dr. Shuch, an education consultant, was tireless in his efforts to encourage us and assist us in conceiving, editing, and publishing the work. We thank him. He can be reached at shelly46@optonline.net.

The authors would also like to thank Rooftop Publishing for believing in *E-Man* and especially Lesley Bolton for her guidance in developing the revised draft for publication.

Contents

Preface xi

Chapter One: The Williamsburg Siege 1

Chapter Two: Hell's Kitchen 13

Chapter Three: 'NAM 21

Chapter Four: The Academy 27

Chapter Five: Last Tour in the 8-1 35

Chapter Six: ESU Training 47

Chapter Seven: The Calls 59

Chapter Eight: The First Time 69

Chapter Nine: The Jumpers 101

Chapter Ten: The Murder of Cecil Sledge 111

Chapter Eleven: Fire, Fear, Death 125

Chapter Twelve: The Day I Killed A Man 135

Chapter Thirteen: Truck 6 Brooklyn South 143

Chapter Fourteen: The Gorilla in the Elevator 151

Chapter Fifteen: Anything but Routine: The Shah of Iran 159

Chapter Sixteen: The Last Midnight 165

Chapter Seventeen: 9/11 175

Epilogue 185

Al Sheppard's Medals and Awards

3 Exceptional Merit Medals

9 Commendation Medals

10 Meritorious Medals

29 Excellent Police Duty Medals

2 Citations for Bravery from the National
Police Officers Association of America

2 Medals from the Seamen's Institute
for saving drowning persons

Letter of Commendation from
Vice President George Bush (1989)

Military Order of the Purple Heart medal
for volunteer work at the World Trade Center
after terrorist attack (2001)

The NYPD Honor Legion Medal (1997)

3 New York Finest Foundation Awards

Preface

My name is Al Sheppard, and during my twenty years as a member of the finest police department in the world, I enjoyed many reputations. For a long time I was known as one of the shortest cops in the department. Toward the end of my career I was the Cult Cop, manning the Devil Desk in the Intelligence Division. I was assigned to investigate crimes of the occult—real boogie-woogie stuff—most of it not founded in reality, but some that left real food for the imagination. Some of the work my partner Jim Tedaldi and I did in the Intelligence Division became the subject of an NBC and Warner Brothers series called *Prince Street*, which was about undercover cops working in the Big Apple.

Eventually, through the connections I made in television, I moonlighted by working in my off hours as a Hollywood stuntman. Most of the time, I got a good laugh about the way Hollywood portrayed our job. But I learned that they also had a job to do. It was about entertainment, not about law enforcement, and it did not necessarily jibe with what we actually did. Most cops loved the show *Barney Miller* as the best cop show on television. I won't argue with that. But in later years, *NYPD Blue* and *Law and Order* became favorites, and I liked *Third Watch*, because it was more about the work I loved the most: rescue work in emergency services.

I was the original technical advisor on *Law and Order* until a difference of opinion got me replaced. My buddy Michael Moriarity, who played the Manhattan DA was very upset. I told him it's all a Hollywood game about personalities. It was not a problem for me. I was never one to kiss ass. That has been one of my problems; I tell it like it is.

I was also a detective in the Major Case Squad. There is no more elite investigative unit in the world of law enforcement. Things happen there that the public never finds out about, even in the cauldron of the New York media. We were battling terrorists before anyone ever heard of Osama Bin Laden and when 9/11 was no different from any other day.

In the 1970s there was Omega 7, a Cuban exile paramilitary terrorist group, and the FALN, the Puerto Rican separatists fighting to free the island from our "imperialist" grip. They were detonating bombs and terrorizing people in ways we are now much more familiar with. They were dangerous bomb makers until William Morales, one of their leaders, blew his own hands and an eye off. I guess what goes around comes around. Imagine that; what a laugh! He was captured and sentenced to a term ranging from twenty-nine to eighty-nine years only to escape while at Bellevue being fitted for artificial limbs. He is now living in Cuba with that other low-life cop killer, Joanne Chesimard.

And don't forget the black Liberation Army's fight against "White man's oppression." They were a small group of militants with virtually no genuine following who knew how to make a lot of noise. They were ruthless, stone-cold killers with cops in their sights. Most ended up where they belonged—dead in the streets with no one to mourn their passing.

Yes, I had a terrific and varied career, but the one assignment I loved the most was working in the Special Operations Division called the Emergency Service Unit, in which we were known as the E-Men. In my own mind—and to the people who know me best, my family, my friends, some newspaper reporters, and to the cops I worked with—I will always be Al Sheppard the E-Man, and that could not make me prouder.

You know those pictures in the newspapers of cops walking up the cables of the Brooklyn Bridge to rescue some poor soul bent on jumping to his death; or of the cop, his face blackened by a recent brush with a burning mattress, carrying an infant out of an inferno; or a cop—weighed down by his bulletproof vest and his round, blue helmet—cradling a shotgun and staring down a dark street toward a sniper's nest? Well, I have done all those things hundreds of times, and so have my E-Man brothers.

I was in a shootout so wild I ran out of ammunition. I have been shot at dozens of times, and once I had to kill a man, as I thought he was about to kill me or my partner, Gary Gorman. I have never second-guessed myself about that. I have not lost sleep over it. It was a matter of life and death. A partner's death is as bad as your own—worse in a way, because you will always wonder if you could have saved him. Any cop I know would do anything possible to save his or her partner.

My actions that night in a Manhattan apartment were instinctive, but I have thought a lot about them since. I am not sure if the experience was a blessing or a curse, but it was certainly what I had to do that night. No doubt!

Few New Yorkers or visitors to the city have not seen those ESU trucks barreling through gridlocked traffic, horns blasting, sirens wailing, and lights flashing while heading toward—always toward—trouble. If Al Sheppard and his partners were called, someone was in trouble.

Most of the time it was a civilian: a teenager struggling to stay afloat in the East River currents, a wounded bodega owner, a suicidal lover, or a family pinned in a wrecked SUV. Sometimes it was a fellow cop in trouble: wounded, pinned down by a psycho, or suffering a heart attack. Or worse, maybe he was already dead.

There is a saying in the NYPD that I am most proud of: "When people need help, they call the police; when the police need help, they call Emergency Services." Nothing explains the pride I had in my work more than those few words.

This memoir is about my work in the Emergency Service Unit. It is a story about courageous men and women putting their own lives at risk for their fellow citizens. It is a story of bravery, foolhardiness, humor, love, despair, fear, and desperation. It is a deeply personal story, because nothing affected my life more than my ten years in the ESU.

Once, I was a hero—a man other brave men looked up to—and I loved it for the most part. But eventually I moved on and decided to put this work behind me. After ten years, I was approaching burnout, and I knew I could still have a promising career ahead of me doing other police work.

My story leads to my last night as an E-Man—a night when I finally came to realize that it was time to move on after rescuing a child from the arms of his mother, who had jumped in front of a moving train.

This is a memoir—my recollections of the way things were, the way people behaved, and the way I felt about things at that time. You may find some reason to disagree with me—a fact, a quote—but remember: it is a story told from the heart.

Chapter One

THE WILLIAMSBURG SIEGE

... The real street of broken dreams

In January 1973, I was a young cop, still wet behind the ears. On the nineteenth of that month, I was working a 4:00 p.m.-to-midnight tour—"four by twelve" in station house jargon—in a radio car in the Eighty-first Precinct. It was a fairly busy house in the Williamsburg section of Brooklyn.

The station house was an old one, even by New York standards. It was more than one hundred years old. It is rumored that during the Civil War, the building was used as a military hospital, so it had seen its share of bloodshed and tears, and if its walls could talk there would be some stories to be told. But none would be as dramatic or heartbreaking as the tale that was to unfold that night in Williamsburg.

The 8-1 was a busy precinct known as the "Hole in the Donut" in the vast patrol area known as Brooklyn North. The area got its nickname because it was a relatively decent part of Brooklyn, as inner-city ghettos go, surrounded on the north by run-down Brownsville, industrial Bushwick to the east, and dangerous Bedford-Stuyvesant to the west. Williamsburg, with its mix of Orthodox Jews, Hispanics, and blacks who had lived there since the end of World War II, was in the southern end of the precinct.

My partner Billy Smith—one of the most veteran black police officers at the time—and I were assigned to sector Adam. The sector bordered the Eighty-third, Seventy-ninth, and Ninetieth precincts.

These were the years during which domestic terrorist groups were beginning to make themselves known to the American public. I'm not talking about the college-based groups, such as the Weathermen or Students for a Democratic Society. What the urban police forces of America were beginning to deal with in these years were the FALN (Puerto Rican separatists), the Black Liberation Army, and the Black Panthers. Not long before this, the Panthers actually had killed a police officer during a traffic stop in Oakland, California, and many police departments, such as those in New York and Chicago, were under attack. This threat was on the mind of every state trooper stopping a car and every undercover cop buying illegal weapons.

One summer night in those years, a mob, led by the Panthers, marched on a Brooklyn precinct, giving the cops a choice of either opening fire to save themselves or retreating behind closed doors and pulling large steel shutters down to cover the windows. This being New York, the cops, press, and civilians barricaded the station house doors and called for help from the Tactical Patrol Force. In fact, the station houses all over the city instituted plans to hold off an attack. At the time, J. Edgar Hoover called the Panthers the greatest threat to freedom we had ever faced. This, of course, was before Al Qaeda.

In NYC, we lost several officers in cowardly ambushes. One was a very good friend and classmate in the police academy named Gregory Foster. He and his partner Rocco Laurie were on foot patrol in the Ninth Precinct on the Lower East Side when they were fatally ambushed, gunned down by automatic weapons. They were simply walking their beat. Foster was a black man, but I guess that didn't matter.

The Black Liberation Army sent out a communiqué saying that the officers were both enemies of the people and part of an occupying army. That could not be further from the truth. Both were devoted to the community. Laurie even paid, from his own pocket, for one local kid to get methadone treatment.

A few months later, two members of the BLA, Woody Green and Avon White, would be shot and killed in the Big T Steakhouse on Broadway in the Eighty-first Precinct by detectives from the Major Case Squad when they resisted rather than go in for questioning in connection with a robbery. The BLA maintained its war chest by pulling off large-scale robberies, and that's why they were under suspicion. They were guilty!

The media was having a difficult time connecting all these various robberies and shootings. I do not believe the public, up to this point, really had an understanding of the mood in the streets, especially in the mean, inner-city neighborhoods.

While no smart cop ever took his patrol for granted, there was an especially tense feeling as we slowly cruised down a street crowded with beat-up cars abandoned in front of once-proud apartment buildings where many of the city's leaders as well as prominent people in many fields—sports, entertainment, politics—had grown up safely in the '40s, '50s, and even into the '60s. By the early '70s in New York City, such neighborhoods were war zones in which drugs were the currency and hate was the politics.

But I was a young cop, a combat vet who was full of piss and vinegar and not afraid of anything. I yearned for hot calls over the radio. I wanted action. I wanted to work. I thought I wanted to make things better for the kids I saw playing in the trash-strewn streets; running errands for drug dealers; and staring blank-eyed into space when we came into their apartments to investigate the drug overdose of their mothers, whose bone-thin bodies would be sprawled out in the next room on a bed made of cardboard.

This night was a typical January—cold and wet. As we settled into our tired green and white Plymouth, our ears tuned to the scratchy voice of the 14th Division dispatcher. In these divisions, covering the kinds of precincts we worked, the dispatcher was a constant companion for eight hours. Night after night she assigned patrol cars to cover jobs generated by 911. We heard everything from a kid with his head caught in a fence to shots fired to reports of officers down. This night was no different: "Shots fired in the 8-3," "Man with a gun in the 9-0," "Stabbing in the 9-4." On and on it would go, all night long, during every tour in Brooklyn North. Violence and despair ruled these streets. But for me, being a cop was still about helping people. I still had the image from my youth of cops coming to the rescue. So, when I looked at the downtrodden in my patrol area, I thought with pride that I was on their side. My job was to help them.

We had handled several routine runs prior to our assigned meal hour. The most exciting involved a dispute between an elderly woman and her grandson, who she said was stealing money from her purse to buy drugs. He had taken offense at the allegation and punched her in the mouth. He had left before we got there, otherwise we might have administered some "street justice." We referred the case to criminal court, but as I left their apartment, I had the thought that someday that addict would kill his grandmother for a taste of dope.

Those kinds of runs ate up time and seemed to take forever. I hated standing in the crowded apartments and feeling so out of place with my gun and nightstick. I thought, *Oh shit! It's going to be a long night.* Nothing made the time drag on more than sitting in a radio car while filling out forms for past crimes, such as complaints against landlords and husbands. No action and all paperwork made for eight-hour tours that felt like eighty hours.

When lunch hour came, because there was no decent place to even get a sandwich in the 14th Division, we sneaked over the borough line into Queens to pick up food and then went back to the precinct to eat it. After we had eaten, we had barely started the engine of the radio motor patrol car (RMP) when we were assigned a 10-30 in a liquor store—a robbery in progress.

The location was not in our sector, but due to a backlog, we were "it." The store was right off Broadway—no, not the Great White Way, the one in Manhattan. This Broadway was the real street of broken dreams. It was littered with garbage, dead rats, broken beer bottles, hypo needles dropped by heroin addicts, and some trash that was just indescribable.

Traffic was heavy. We hit the lights and siren, and then, as per procedure, we shut it all down a few blocks from the location. No need to advertise our arrival to the bad guys.

For some reason, I remember that as we were driving, I was thinking of my first month in the precinct, about two years earlier, when my partner and I had turned a corner and driven right by a shooting.

We were on our way to a 10-52 domestic. While turning off of Broadway at Chauncey Street, a man shot another man in the head right in front of us. The victim literally fell onto the hood of our RMP. The street was full of people, and dozens of children were running in all directions. We jumped out of the car and, with guns drawn, took cover behind its doors. We shouted to the man with the gun, telling him to drop it.

We were in a Mexican standoff. But the rules were unfair; we couldn't fire because of the chance of hitting a civilian. It lasted maybe a minute, but it felt like an hour. He finally attempted to fire, but his automatic pistol jammed. We were on him like stink on shit. We took him down hard to the street, all to the cheers of the crowd.

We later learned that killing involved a decade-old dispute between two cousins. One ended up dead; the other did hard time upstate.

That was a routine call that ended in terror-filled moments. We were headed for the same thing tonight, only I did not know it yet. Of course, I would welcome any action—the more dangerous, the better. Or so I thought.

As we approached the location, we saw "Old Sal" waving his arms. He had the usual cigar clenched between his teeth. Sal was a tough old Jewish man from Brownsville. It was rumored that he had been associated with Murder Inc.—the Prohibition-era mob run by the likes of Meyer Lansky, Lucky Luciano, and Bugsy Seigel.

I loved learning about guys like "Old Sal" because I had always been a student of New York history, especially its criminal history. Murder Incorporated began as a murder-for-hire outfit in which the young Jewish mobsters earned their spurs by working on retainer deals, getting paid while they waited for assignments. Eventually it earned its rep under the leadership of Albert Anastasia, who was shot to death sitting in his barber chair, and Louis "Lepke" Buchalter, who died in the chair at Sing Sing.

Despite his notorious background, Sal was a super guy, and he was always happy to see the cops. The clerk in the liquor store told us the perp was long gone. My partner, Billy Smith, as I have said, was an old-timer—one of the first black cops to be assigned to a radio car beat—and he knew the clerk. They greeted each other by their first names. Billy, who had maybe twenty years' seniority on me, told me to go back and sit in the RMP. I took his cue, recalling the way my platoon sergeant in 'Nam would always take control of situations the same way.

In the car, I lit a cigarette and sat back and listened to the nonstop voice of the dispatcher. No doubt about it, things were heating up. I began to think it might be a busy night after all.

Looking into the liquor store through its large windows, I saw Sal smiling and the clerk and my partner in a brotherly bear hug.

The radio droned on job after job—shots fired in the 8-3, a recorded holdup alarm in the 9-0 at John & Al's Sporting Goods Store. These were not unusual calls; we got them all the time like clockwork.

Then, in a moment that has stood still in my memory all these years, I heard a voice gasping for breath and trying to scream over the radio, "10-13, 10-13, officer shot, Myrtle and Broadway." I could actually hear gunfire in the background. *Shit*, I thought. *That's our sector, where it borders the Ninetieth Precinct.* That's where the sporting goods store was.

I jumped out of the RMP and ran into the store, yelling, "We got a cop shot at Myrtle and Broadway!" As we ran back to the car, my heart was beating as if it was going to explode in my chest.

We did what dozens of cops throughout Brooklyn were doing at that very second. We hit the lights and siren and raced to the scene. But unlike most of those other cops, we were close—only about eight blocks away. Not unexpectedly, Billy was a great driver. It is drummed into you in drivers' training that you should never make things worse by getting into a crash on the way to the crime. We were there in a minute or so, but it seemed to take longer.

We pulled into the northeast corner of the intersection, facing opposing traffic. Gunfire was sounding through the streets. Unbelievably, the RMP was taking rounds, so both of us bailed out of the driver-side door and onto the wet, cold street. I crawled under the car and emptied my service revolver in the direction of the store. Maybe it wasn't the smartest thing to do since I had no idea of who was shooting at who, but I did not want anyone thinking of me as an easy target.

My combat vet instincts told me these were high-powered rounds being fired at us. Since John & Al's was a sporting goods store, anyone inside would have had access to all sorts of weapons and ammo, and as we later found out, there were also hostages. Police from the Seventy-ninth, Eighty-third, and Ninetieth precincts had responded when a holdup alarm was tripped, and they were now caught in a resulting shootout. Looking around, I could see there were three officers down, wounded and unable to get to cover. As I surveyed the scene, I also saw at least six other radio cars with cops pinned down behind them.

A subway train went rumbling overhead, adding to the nightmare. More and more cops were arriving, but they were unable to get past the police cars already there. One cop was brave enough to stand up and wave to the others to stop. Over the radio, I could hear another cop from my precinct trying to explain to dispatch what the hell was going on.

"Multiple officers down, we need emergency service, we need buses [ambulances, in police jargon], perps barricaded in John & Al's . . . 10-13, 10-13."

Another cop had the presence of mind to clear the street of civilians; he was using his body to protect them as they ran down Broadway across the street from John & Al's.

Meanwhile, central dispatch was trying to get some handle on the situation.

"Any unit in the 8-1, how many down, how many down? How many perps? Are there civilians injured? What is the status?"

Finally, an 8-1 sergeant got on the air and calmed the dispatcher a little.

"This is a serious firefight; we need citywide mobilization. Alert all officers responding to use extreme caution."

I heard all this while trying to make myself invisible under the car.

We were in a world of shit, as the first sergeant had said during the beginning of the Tet Offensive just a few short years before.

But that was in a jungle in Southeast Asia, and our country was at war. This was happening in the middle of New York City.

During a break in the firing, a sergeant yelled to me to run for cover behind the elevated subway pole in front of the Oasis Bar, which was across from the sporting goods store. Taking cover behind the RMP was now useless. The perps, who had a store that was full of ammo, were firing under the cars. I made a dash and sat back against the steel pole. The front door and windows of the bar were riddled with bullet holes. Billy followed and also made it.

This was the same bar used in the movie *The French Connection*. I thought it strange, because Eddie "Popeye" Egan was a detective in the 8-1 squad, and they fashioned Gene Hackman's movie character after him. Now was a good time to reload. I still had eighteen rounds of .38 caliber ammo and eight 9mm rounds in my backup Smith & Wesson. The subway trains were still rumbling ten feet above us. We couldn't hear the radio or each other.

There it was again, the transit authority taking its time shutting down power. No matter what, the trains had to run. They ran for another ten minutes while the NYPD hid under cars. When they stopped, the only sounds were the sporadic gunfire that echoed through the cold night.

My brother officers still lay in the street, unable to move. Every time someone moved, his motion was met with a burst of automatic weapon fire coming from within the darkened store. A voice came over the radio; it was a sergeant ordering us to shoot out the streetlight—undoubtedly the first time an order like that was ever given to a New York cop. But we were sitting ducks while silhouetted by the street lamps. As each light was shot out, the thick glass crashed to the ground.

I called over to a nearby cop. I thought that if he could cover me, I could crawl over to the cop closest to us and try to drag him to safety. His reply was stern: "Kid, don't be a hero; a hero is nothing but a sandwich. ESU will be here any minute."

Indeed, Truck 8 was on its way; sirens and air horns could be heard in the distance. I had no way of knowing it that night while about fifty other cops and I were pinned down under the elevated trains, but about ten years later, Truck 8 would be my last assignment in my beloved ESU.

As I looked down the street, I saw the enormous truck pull to the curb. It was painted green, black, and white—the color scheme of the NYPD. Large green letters on a white background proclaimed "Police Emergency Squad."

Peering through the cold mist, I could make out about eight men suited up in bulky bulletproof vests and carrying heavy weapons. They were here to save us.

It's not my original thought, but I came to live by the well-known adage, "When a civilian needs help, he calls the police; when the police need help, they call ESU." How true that was then, and it remains so today with the new breed of the men and women of the finest and most diverse police force in the world. And these days, their responsibilities have grown to include the battle of international terrorists.

On that night in Williamsburg, many of the police department's field commanders were Korean War veterans, and some even dated back to World War II. Many of the pinned-down cops, like me, were Vietnam vets. We were a seasoned bunch, even rookies like me. I watched as the commanders arrived in their bright, unmarked cars, which were driven by sergeants. I knew they would never venture into the ghettos unless absolutely necessary. They had a calming effect on the whole scene. I bet even the perpetrators were glad to see a command post being set up a block away. Maybe some gray-haired, old Irish guy who survived the Chosin Reservoir in Korea would figure a way out of this mess.

Over the years, cities throughout the nation, and indeed the world, would develop SWAT teams. While the NYPD, ever mindful of a liberal constituency, never had such a designated unit, most of those SWAT teams were based on the strategy and tactics developed by the NYPD Special Operations Division, of which the ESU is a unit.

I watched in awe, therefore, as these emergency service guys pulled up to the nightmarish scene. There were cops lying under cars and civilians screaming and running around in panic while the radio chatter from the RMP radios filled the air with the urgent voices of cops and dispatchers trying to organize things until these ESU guys finally took over. Their calm, professional attitude brought some semblance of control to the scene, which now covered about five blocks. They seemed to know what to do without being told, and that had a beneficial effect on everyone involved. I met some of them that night—guys like ESS Captain Dennis Healy, ESS 9 Sergeant Ed Leighs, ESS 2 Jack Casey, ESS 2 Frank Gallagher, and ESS 2 Ken Jaques, all of who became lifelong friends. They are people I always tried to pattern myself after as I learned the job.

The ESU officers positioned themselves all around us. One of them dashed to position himself behind an elevated pole directly in front of the entrance to John & Al's. All this time, gunfire continued to pour from inside the darkened store.

Then, in a moment frozen in my mind forever, I watched one of the most honorable actions I had ever seen unfold outside of actual wartime combat. The officer behind the pole moved to his right, trying to get a better angle into the shop in order to lay down some fire so the rest of the pinned-down cops could scamper to cover. He had taken about two steps when he was gunned down; it was a fatal hit, no doubt about it.

His name was Stephen Gilroy. There is a plaque honoring this hero in the quarters of Truck 8. The day came when I walked past it every time I reported to duty. And every time, it would bring back the smell of that wet cobblestone street, the fear and anger that we patrol cops felt, and the frustration of watching Gilroy fall.

We were pinned down for almost two hours, with the firing finally reduced to an occasional shot from the store every few minutes, when I noticed from the corner of my eye flashbulbs popping and television camera people scurrying for position. Also in the background was a rumbling sound I had not heard since 'Nam. It was coming closer.

There was no mistake about it. That was the sound of an armored personnel carrier; its tracks chewing up the city streets. It was a vehicle we had heard about but never seen. Not long before this night, Police Commissioner Patrick V. Murphy had announced the department had purchased a "rescue ambulance."

We laughed when we heard about it. The liberal Murphy would not call it an armored personnel carrier (APC), which is what it was; in New York, "rescue ambulance" was much more acceptable. As if that made any sense! But no matter what you called it, it was our ticket out of harm's way.

In fairness, I have to admit that on that evening, it did perform as Murphy advertised. The "rescue ambulance" jockeyed itself into position in front of the sporting goods store. As it blocked the windows and door, cops were able to reach Gilroy's body and the other injured officers. We pinned-down cops ran alongside the APC, out of the killing zone and into a bank building down the street that had been turned into a temporary headquarters. I remember seeing Police Commissioner Murphy inside. There we were in our now filthy, wet, stinky uniforms, standing in a room with the impeccable Murphy. I may not have agreed with his politics, but I was impressed by his commanding figure. He was clearly in charge.

We were debriefed by a deputy chief and, sadly, sent back to our precincts. We did not want to leave. We had watched a fellow officer get shot to death, and others were wounded. We wanted to finish the job. But the bosses said they had it under control, and they knew we were fatigued. A tired cop could make a mistake that could cost him or his partner his life.

The arrival of Murphy's tank stopped the shooting. The perps must have shit their pants, thinking they could get blown away by a tank gun (they did not know there was no gun on the vehicle). The situation became a hostage negotiation that lasted through the night and for three more days.

Later we heard in the station house that the hostages escaped after the ESU effected entry into the store via the roof and was able to rescue them. There to lead them to safety were the E-Men of Truck 2, which was led by Jack Case and Bobby Benz—some of my heroes—and Frank Gallagher, who drove the APC.

Faced with cops on the roof and even more in the streets, the four Sunni Muslim gunmen surrendered forty-seven hours after the initial alarm was sent, although they did so reluctantly after having killed one of our own. They walked out of the store with their fists raised in defiance, and that set the mood in the neighborhood for weeks to come.

As the perps were handcuffed and led away, hundreds of people began throwing bottles and breaking windows. The streets were full of hatred for the cops. The media combed the streets, looking for eyewitnesses and inciting more trouble wherever they turned their flashbulbs and camera lights. Commissioner Murphy tried to tell the story of the death of E-Man Stephen Gilroy, but it was overtaken by a bullshit story of rebellion. These perps were bandits, not revolutionaries.

In the cop bars that evening and for many evenings after, we rehashed the incident. Most thought we should have just blown away the scumbags, too bad for the hostages. A lot of guys took on some anger that night and may still be living with it.

But I personally took something a little different away from that night. I knew that my future lay with the ESU.

And within two years, my dream came true; I got my first assignment to Truck 4 in the Bronx.

Chapter Two

HELL'S KITCHEN

... The cop on the beat would make sure your parents knew you had a scrap

I grew up on New York's west side in Midtown, that part of the city roughly between Fifty-seventh Street on the north, Thirty-fourth Street on the south, Eighth Avenue on the east, and the Hudson River on the west. These days it is called "Clinton" and is a part of the explosion of prosperity that has come about with the rebirth of Times Square. Today it is a neighborhood of trendy restaurants, bars that serve apple martinis, occasional boutiques, and new luxury high-rises that are squeezing out the century-old tenements where my friends and I grew up when the neighborhood was known as "Hell's Kitchen." I'm not against progress, and God knows that what is there now is better than the porn shops and skin shows that saturated the area during the '70s and '80s. We certainly have to thank Rudy Giuliani and his tough backing of Bill Bratton for that.

The neighborhood was the model for movies starring Jimmy Cagney as a tough kid hoodlum; the dead end kids could have been my classmates. The adults in the neighborhood were, for the most part,

13

second-generation Irish, mostly civil servants and laborers, lowly paid but learning about the values of unions and good pensions.

I lived in a five-story walk up, or a cold-water flat. We did not have hot water unless we boiled the cold water to make some. We lived on the top floor. It was murder when my mom, Virginia, who was born in Trenton, New Jersey, went shopping. This was before the big supermarket days. She would go to one store for some things, a baker, a butcher, and maybe to the A&P, and I had to carry those bags up the five flights of stairs to our apartment.

While I was growing up, she worked down the street in the Long Distance department of the telephone company. In the 1960s, she did a remarkable thing: she went back to school and became a teacher. After retirement she lived with her second husband Tom Tuscano, a guy from the Little Italy section of East Harlem who was a union boss on the old New York Central. Sadly Mom passed away in 2007.

Mrs. Snyder, an elderly Jewish woman who lived in the building but never came out of her apartment, had her own unique style of going shopping. She would lower a basket with a grocery list and money in an envelope out of her first-floor window. I would be waiting outside to take it to the Zingonie grocery, which was owned by the only Italians in the neighborhood. When I brought the groceries back, I would ring her bell and leave the groceries by her door. On the mat outside the door, there would be a nickel or dime. This was a weekly ritual.

Our apartment was called a railroad flat. There were windows between each room. I guess that gave it the appearance of a railroad car. As a kid, I could never figure that out. The neighborhood was mostly Irish and German, with a few Jewish families. There were no blacks, but the Hispanic population was growing fast. I don't know how we survived summer without air conditioning. I would sleep on the fire escape with a blanket. I would stare up at the stars and hear Gershwin's "Rhapsody in Blue" in my mind. George and Ira were my favorites.

In the winter, we would freeze. When we got out of bed we could actually see our breath. Mom would hang my pants on the stove door overnight so I could slip into them in the morning. There is nothing like sliding into warm pants. Years later, I would think of that every time

I had to make a quick uniform change in the cold emergency service garage.

When I was a kid, we didn't have our own bathroom. It was in the hallway, and it was shared by the three families that lived on each floor. They called it a water closet. My bathtub was in the kitchen, and it had metal covers on top of it. There was one television in the entire building. Everyone would flock to the Campbells' apartment at night to see Jack Parr and Uncle Milty. There were two phones in the building. I remember the phone number: Susquehanna 7-5474. The building reminded me of Jackie Gleason's apartment on *The Honeymooners*.

In those days, people were not on welfare. It was called home relief. If the City found a person on home relief with a telephone or television, *boom!* they were in the soup! I can recall coming home one day from P.S. 9, my elementary school, and seeing my friend's entire apartment out on the street in front of the building. Even their bird cage was outside, with the bird still in it. My friend's parents had missed a rent payment. Later in the day, the Old Westies, as the local gang was known, came and paid the rent for the family. The original Westies were not what Mickey Featherstone and his crew became—basically a bunch of murderous thugs. The Old Westies were like Robin Hood—mostly into numbers and loan sharking. But you knew not to cross them.

I grew up with many of the Westies, and years later I saw them a lot when working on the television and movie stuff. Most are associated with a big company that specializes in moving sets for the Broadway theaters around town. They can shut down a production if they choose to, so they carry a lot of clout with the producers. In the 1980s, to their everlasting disgrace, they joined up with the Gambino crime family; actually, they became lackeys and gofers for John Gotti and the Italian mobsters. More often than not, the Westies members were drug users and drunks, and they ended up killing each other. They were finally pretty much broken up by the legendary Sergeant Joe Coffey and the NYPD's organized crime detectives. These days, they are a peaceful sort.

My father's name was Watt Sheppard. He was a boss in the machinists union. He worked for Berlin & Jones on West Eighteenth Street and Twelfth Avenue. He is one of New York City's oldest printers and envelope makers. He was very good friends with the famous civil rights lawyer Paul O'Dwyer. I remember staring at the great man's brilliant white hair and his famous bushy eyebrows. Dad also had some organized crime guys among his friends. I guess that was common for union leaders in New York in those days.

My dad grew up in western Virginia, had worked in the coal mines, and was a big union supporter. The first Sheppards were two brothers who left Banff, Scotland around 1730 to settle in Fredericksburg, Virginia. They left their parents, a sister, and a brother behind. I figure that they had problems with the English. They both became successful planters. The next generation moved to Wilksboro, North Carolina. My great-great-grandfather was a Confederate private in the 36th Virginia Infantry. All his brothers served with the 26th North Carolina.

Dad never lost his southern accent, and so he was known as The Rebel. During labor disputes, he was the expert at throwing boxes of steel ball bearings off the loading docks and letting them fall along the cobblestone streets of Twelfth Avenue while waiting there for the mounted cops, or "mounties," to come. Those little ball bearings would play havoc with the horses' hooves. The poor animals would slip, and sometimes fall, as their riders tried to maneuver them into the picket lines.

Years later, the antiwar demonstrators would employ the same tactics, and I would be one of those mounties for a short time while serving in ESU. I always laughed to myself when swinging my nightstick down on one of the demonstrators. *They needed The Rebel to show them how to do that,* I would think.

My dad's friends were firefighters, postal workers, construction guys, cops, and stevedores on the docks. All of them were war veterans of Korea or WWII. They played softball over on Eleventh Avenue, drank and gambled in bars whose names all began with O' something or other. They fought with their fists, they were tough on their wives and kids, and they generally believed that the railroad flat where their several children shared a bedroom and all lined up for the bathroom was a far cry better than what their own parents had. Sports were the center of my life growing up. I lived and ate baseball, but I also boxed and played football in the Bronx Federation League. And I am proud to say that I was a member of the Wollman Rink speed skating team. The Wollman Ice Rink in Central Park is a jewel of New York.

If you asked the young Al Sheppard what he wanted to be when he grew up, the answer would be the same as that of thousands of other American kids: a ballplayer. I played baseball and football wherever I could find a game, such as in the Puerto Rican League in Central Park. I traveled to the Bronx to play in the Federation League at Babe Ruth Field, across the street from Yankee Stadium, and I played in Frisch Field, in the East Bronx. I also played football in the Bronx Federation League. I played at Charles Evans Hughes High School, where the coach was Joe Levine, a man who played a very supportive role in my life at the time. He thought I was a good baseball player and wanted me to go to Fordham University. He was a guy who knew that playing ball kept active young men out of trouble. I made varsity during my freshman year, 1965, which was an achievement because Hughes High School was the PSAL city champ in baseball. I was even selected to the All-City team. I got a tryout with the Chicago White Sox, but they were not impressed, even though I played against some guys who would go on to the majors, such as Ed Kranepool of the New York Mets.

It did not appear that I would be one of them, but deep inside I guess I did not have the confidence to go further. I thought the major leagues were an impossible dream, and so as my senior year approached, I started thinking about alternatives to college. I tried to join the marines, but they discovered I was only seventeen. My father was pissed off. He wanted me to continue in school. In between all that playing, I did find time to hold down some part-time jobs. I had a paper route that covered all the bars on Tenth Avenue from the low forties to the seventies. I'd go to Grand Central Terminal to buy the *Daily News* and the *New York Post* in bulk. They were a penny cheaper that way. I had regular clients. Everyone waited for the late edition to see what number came out. Actually, it was a very profitable operation. My buddy and I got at least five cents and usually twenty-five cents from the barflies. And if one hit the number, you were sure to get between one and five dollars for being the bearer of good news.

In addition to my newspaper job, I worked at the candy store before school. I'd pull out the wooden floorboards from behind the counter, take them outside, and mop them off. Then I would go to the basement and sort out two-cent and five-cent bottles. I did this every morning for ten dollars a week plus a free ten-cent seltzer. And if I was lucky, I would get a lime ricky—a drink that anyone living in the city at that time would remember.

So, in my senior year of high school, anxious to get out into the world and with my baseball career not going the way I wanted, I decided to take the test for the police academy. I had already joined the academy's cadet program—an entryway into the NYPD that would look great on my record—so I saw the police department as a way out.

My father, who died in 1973, hated cops. He called them "grafting heathens." He hated that some could be bought off, and he was filled with rage at the mounted cops who were called in to break up picket lines. "Most times, those Broadway producers could treat the 'grafting heathens' better than the working men," he would say. But I had always admired cops. I remember getting swatted on the backside by a couple of them from time to time. It didn't bother me. Of course, the cop on the beat would make sure your parents knew you had a scrap. Sometimes Dad would take out the strap and finish what the cop started. But my friends and I did not resent this. We took our medicine and moved on, especially because we knew we deserved it.

I even witnessed two shootouts in my neighborhood, and I came away in awe of the way the men in blue handled themselves. They were full of self-assurance. They were disciplined and determined. We all looked up to them—except, of course, my father. And I had an uncle in the ESU, Sergeant Bill Monahan. I would visit him on Saturday mornings. The Eighteenth Precinct, which is now Midtown North, was the quarters of an emergency service unit, and my uncle would let me climb around the ancient truck, which was chock full of things kids love, such as ropes, ladders, and some other rudimentary rescue equipment.

My uncle was also a good friend of Jack Dempsey, who was a first cousin of my grandmother from County Kildare, Ireland. The champ owned a famous restaurant in the precinct. We would go there for lunch on the weekends, and Jack would always welcome us and sit at our table for a while. My friends envied me because of this in a big way. Many years later, when the champ was dying and I was a cop, I visited him in the hospital. There was a cop guarding his door, courtesy of a loving city, but when he heard little Al Sheppard was waiting outside, he asked them to let me in. He remembered my uncle. He was proud of me becoming a cop. I was one of the last people to speak with him. He died a few days later. What a great man!

With all this going on—baseball, work, and visiting the Manassa Mauler—my high school life was drawing to an end. It was the police department for me. So I took the test. I couldn't afford to go to Delahanty's, where many of us learned the tricks of passing civil service exams, so I studied the ARCO book at night in the Eighteenth Precinct with Sergeant Al Toefield helping me. He was my mentor. He had played pro ball with the New York Giants, and everyone looked up to him. But instead of waiting to get my results (I never was very patient), I decided to join the army.

Looking back on those years, I remember New York as a much simpler place, a more innocent place than it is today. I suppose the big changes came along with the scourge of drugs and its sisters, prostitution and death, but perhaps all of us remember the past as "the good old days." Of course, I was to become intimate with the worst of New York. I would learn what it was like to face down a killer. I would see firsthand the ravages of poverty. I would hold dying homeless men in my arms and save deranged grandmothers from killing themselves.

The warmth, the love, and the security of the days in Hell's Kitchen quickly faded into my memory, but thankfully, not from my heart.

Chapter Three

'NAM

. . . And even The Rebel was proud as could be

I don't talk much about my tour in Vietnam. Like my varied and often-failed love life, Vietnam was something I went into determined to do well, and it ended up in a world of shit. I was going nowhere in high school. I was a smart kid, but if you watched me in the classroom, you would have thought I had the heebie-jeebies. There is a great Yiddish word, *shpilkus*, that means "ants in the pants." That was me. I could not wait to get going and to get the world by the balls. I never thought the world would get me by the balls.

I tried to join the marines at seventeen, but the dumb-looking gunny at the recruiting station was not as dumb as he looked, and they found me out and sent me home. My dad, a World War II Seabee who left a lung and a large piece of his leg in the Pacific, could not understand why I wanted to get my ass shot off in Vietnam, but he did understand my thirst for adventure. While a senior in high school, I took the test for the police academy cadet program—an entryway into the NYPD that would look great on my record—but before I heard back from them, I joined the army. Most of the guys I know who have survived combat do not like to talk about it. The same goes for me. But I have chosen to write a memoir, and that year in the jungle was certainly memorable. Most of the heavy fighting I was involved in is a blur. I remember feelings of raw terror followed by unbelievable relief, often feeling my fate was out of my control and then understanding that if I controlled myself, I could possibly control whether or not I survived a particular circumstance. This was knowledge that would serve me very well on the mean streets of Brooklyn and the Bronx. My natural ability to focus on a dangerous situation and concoct a solution was not unlike Joe Namath's ability to clear his mind of distractions on the field and pick out the receiver. It came naturally, but it was honed in 'Nam.

I learned things about my fellow man that would serve me well in my future in law enforcement. I learned that some men were intrinsically bad, selfish, and even sociopathic. They were similar to some I would be locking up in the future. I also learned that some men were angels walking on the earth; they were selfless and willing to throw themselves on hand grenades to save their fellow soldiers. Some would give their last ration to a native kid who hadn't eaten that day. But most were like me—we did our job just to get through the day. There were some things I did that others may call heroic, but I was just doing my duty. Like everyone else, I wanted to get home, get married, get a job, raise a family, and most of all, try to forget how horrible war can be.

During basic training, the army put on a show with its airborne and Army Special Forces troops, and it convinced me and two buddies to join the airborne forces. Right after basic training, we were in Fort Campbell, Kentucky, home of the Screaming Eagles. We thought we were the coolest dudes on earth, especially after completing the first week, which was basically running all day. I needed to build up my legs, lungs, and the spirit of camaraderie that would carry us through the difficult times ahead and, later in life, would serve me very well in the NYPD.

The second week of airborne training was "Tower Week." That was when we were taught how to properly set up our chutes, how to roll on impact with the ground, and how to jump from towers at various heights—all high. But of course, none of that compares to the day when you make your first jump, which is called a "Cherry Blast." Here I am, eighteen years old, a neighborhood kid from Hell's Kitchen, and I am standing in line in the belly of a cargo plane with guys from all over the country, wearing the fatigues of the 101st Airborne Division—the heroes of Normandy and the Battle of the Bulge and of the commanding officer currently in Iraq, General David H. Petraeus—and we're waiting to jump into 1800 feet of air.

Let me tell you—and anyone who has ever done that will tell you the same—we were scared shitless, but we did it. I was terrified as the jump master shouted, "Stand up, hook up, move to the door." I was about tenth in line, but I would have preferred to be first. That way I would not have had time to think about it. Instead I watched nine teenagers disappear through the door before it was my turn. I never doubted I would jump when the time came. I would not humiliate myself in front of the other trainees. And so, with my heart racing and my stomach in my throat, I went out the door. I closed my eyes, screamed, and gripped the handle on my reserve chute as if my life depended on it. I fell at 100 mph for the longest time, and then I was jerked upwards as my chute opened and filled with air. I guess the line on my chute worked, because I never pulled the reserve chute open. I prayed and prayed until I realized I was floating and I could not hear the engines of the plane. I could hear nothing but the wind rushing through my helmet.

Up to that point in my life, I had never felt so alive or accomplished. I remember thinking, *This is great, this is fuckin' great! I wish the gang on Columbus Avenue could see me now.* After a perfect roll upon landing and the recovery of my chute, I was on my way to airborne graduation, the privilege of wearing that nifty special badge on my uniform, and—of course—the wings of a paratrooper.

When jump school ended, we had our graduation and marched around looking and acting like we were the greatest warriors who ever marched on this earth. We all knew, of course, we were headed for Vietnam. But first we got leave, and I went home for two weeks. Coincidentally, my old pal Ronnie Alphonso was also home on leave. He had just finished a tour in 'Nam. We had been friends from P.S. 9 through high school. We often talked about being partners on the police force together: crime fighters, the scourge of the black hearted, John Wayne and Errol Flynn fighting the mobsters.

That was our dream, and Ronnie was already on the way, having been accepted to the police cadets even before he joined the service, like I had been. I told him I was on the police department list but that I did not know if I would be called before it expired. But there was a chance for our boyhood dreams to come true. We partied for two weeks, always returning to that theme of how we would work together, watch each other's backs, and take care of each other's families.

What ruined the dream was that you had to be twenty-one to be on the force, and Ronnie did not make it. While he was home, he found out that his girlfriend was pregnant. He wanted to be with her, but he still had more than two years to serve. It was breaking his heart. But he knew that if he volunteered to go back to 'Nam for a second tour, he could shave some time off his remaining service. He volunteered. When he left Hell's Kitchen he promised to look me up "in country," as the war zone was called. Well, he never looked me up. You know where this is going. Two weeks later, he was dead. We never patrolled the South Bronx together. His kid never knew his father.

Once "in country" with my unit, we were taken to a training camp, where we were shown all of the Viet Congs' tricks. It was the ten-cent tour of what to expect and be on the alert for: bungee sticks, tripwires, and hand grenades suspended in trees over our heads. The camouflaged pits lined with bamboo spikes also gave me nightmares. Imagine a nice handsome boy like me falling into one of those . . . ugh!

I remembered my dad's words the day I left home: "You'll change your mind about this war once the lead starts flying," The Rebel had told me. Dad was against the war. He hated the antiwar protesters, but inside, he hated war more. Having been there, he did not want his son to go. After that training camp, as we waited for our assignment to a command, we would see the steel coffins and listen to the stories of the guys on their way home. I did not doubt my abilities. I was well trained. But before I even faced a shot fired in anger, I wondered what the hell I had gotten myself into. What the hell were we doing there? Dad could be right about some things.

I spent a year remembering those words. It was a year spent, as we used to say, "in the shit." I saw men—boys, really—die, and I did my share of returning the favor. My unit distinguished itself. Like I said, I don't like to talk or think much about my time in 'Nam. Just know that the 101st had the third-highest losses of any ground unit, and it would have been even higher had we been fully mobilized earlier—you can look it up. When I eventually hit the street that night in Williamsburg, I was prepared for the agony ahead by what one year in Vietnam did for me.

Then, while sitting in the jungle one day, I got mail stating that I had been accepted to the police academy. That allowed me to leave the service early, and as soon as I was finished in 'Nam, I was discharged so I could become an officer in the NYPD. Was I happy? Can an eagle fly?

My father would not acknowledge my achievement. But after a year on the job, I made the front page of the *New York Post* for the arrest of a guy who shot two cops in Brooklyn. I was a hero in the city, and that included Hell's Kitchen. And even The Rebel was as proud as any father could be.

Chapter Four

THE ACADEMY

. . . Shepp to the rescue

So the long-awaited day came when I reported to the New York Police Department's Department of Personnel for my physical and my agility test. I needed to pass this test before I could actually report for training at the police academy on East Twenty-first Street. The Department of Personnel was way downtown from my apartment, but because of the way that the west side of Manhattan eventually merges with the east side, it was a direct subway ride, then a short walk, and I was there.

On the subway, I took close notice of a transit authority cop walking his beat through the rumbling, shaking train car. In those days, the transit authority had a separate police force, although they worked hand in hand with the NYPD. It was not the kind of police work I envisioned for myself. These transit cops may have been the city's most courageous law enforcement personnel, as they had to patrol the dark, dirty subways alone, with radios that hardly communicated with the surface. I thought they were confined and trapped, despite the constant movement along the tracks. I yearned for the wide-open streets, like Broadway, that ran above the subway line, where I could barrel along in an emergency truck, racing to save someone's life or maybe rescue a cop in trouble. I wanted to climb bridges and scale buildings with the eyes of the city upon me: Shepp to the rescue!

When it was time to take a physical, I was ready for any test they could hand out. After all, I was shortly out of the 101st Airborne Division, the Screaming Eagles. I had mastered the art of combat parachuting and I had survived the shit—"fucking 'Nam man," as the emerging hippie musicians were saying. I had never been in better shape in my life.

The physical and agility test was an all-day affair. I arrived at 7:00 a.m. sharp, full of piss and vinegar. When I exited the elevator, I was amazed at the sight that awaited me. Up and down the narrow hallway were guys about my age, some a little older, who were engaged in bizarre exercises aimed at gaining or losing a pound or two or growing an inch or two at the last minute.

Some fit young men were eating bananas by the bunch, gulping down jugs of water, or running in place and doing calisthenics. Others were doing some things that suddenly hit home to me. It had never seemed a problem to me before, but I was a short guy—just about 5' 7" on the nose, which was the minimum height, in those days, for being accepted as a cop. My height was never a handicap to me. As a ballplayer, I patrolled the middle infield, where short guys were common. On the gridiron, I was a compact halfback, hard to bring down because of my strong legs and proximity to the ground. In the airborne, no one held my height against me as long as I could run the backbreaking endurance courses and hold my own in the bar fights in the small towns outside our base. Being short in a jungle was actually an advantage. Enemy rounds soared over my head, and my trips to the bunker were faster than those of the big, gangly guys. But now I was seeing otherwise healthy young men being carried in on boards by their friends amid talk of how they had slept on the floor for the past week. One applicant was actually hitting himself on top of the head with a small ball peen hammer, hoping, I guess, that they would measure the bump it caused.

Eventually, we were lined up just like we had been at the Whitehall Street Induction Center when I joined the army—standing in a long line wearing nothing but our underwear and socks. But now I was worried about the height thing. I was worrying myself. *Maybe I should have slept on the floor; maybe I should have let my hair grow; maybe I should have worn my combat boots; maybe I should stand at attention, chest out, back straight. Maybe I should never have smoked a cigarette.*

I was about three recruits away from the ancient scale that would decide my fate. The scale was equipped with a plate on top that had a handle, which was dropped to the top of your head. If you were height and weight qualified, two green lights would come on. If not, you were sent home.

I watched as one applicant was ordered to get off the scale and remove his socks. The room erupted in laughter when it was exposed that he had taped lifts to his heels. The short guy was left in humiliation. *Oh shit!* I thought. I never thought I was too short for the force. I was sure I was 5′7″, or was I? My heart pounded. "Next, Sheppard, get up on the scale." I closed my eyes and started to stretch my neck. I never saw the lights. "Okay," the man said, "go to the next station." I was soon to become one of the shortest cops in the NYPD.

I entered the academy in November 1970. Most of our class members were former police trainees who had served at police headquarters as telephone clerks and other office workers. On the first day, we were taken to the property clerk's office at 400 Broome Street. It reminded me of boot camp. Everyone lined up with a large paper bag, only this time we had clothes on. In boot camp, your first stop was the oversized boxer shorts, then a T-shirt, and so on. This was finished when you were in full boot dress. Here on Broome Street, we were first issued our shields (and by the way, we had to pay fifteen cents out of our own pockets for the pins). That's something I'll never forget. You had to pay for *everything*. Actually, every NYPD rookie had to pay for everything. The only thing the NYPD gave you was your shield. And it wasn't yours; it was the property of the NYPD. But it was an NYPD shield, and it was issued to you. What a proud moment for me.

There came a time I accurately traced my shield number. I met Lieutenant Dempsey, an attorney assigned to the advocate's office on Centre Street. He told me he was the second NYPD officer to have the shield, 1177. I was number three. I asked what happened to the first guy.

He replied, "I think he was a German in the early turn of the century; got killed in a robbery or something like that."

We were given a loan to pay for our uniforms and weapons, and we were told we could only go to "authorized" tailors. I always wondered how the tailors got picked. But Smith & Grey were reported to be the best, so that's where I went. At that time, the rookie uniforms were gray; only the eight-pointed hat was blue. Kind of made you stand out to say the least. I was all hyped up because I got to be in a uniform and have a gun strapped to my waist.

My instructor was Anthony Gambino, a lieutenant and a real gentleman. Don't let the name fool you; he was no relation to the Mafia's Gambinos. I was fortunate enough to work with him toward the end of a career two decades later. I still remember his first words to Company B. "Look around you," he said, and then there he paused. "Take a real good look. Some of you will not make the grade. Some of you will quit after a short time. Some of you will get killed, some arrested, and some will strive to a great career. Remember the three Bs—booze, broads, bucks. The three Bs will end your career in a heartbeat."

I was determined not to fall into those traps, but I always had a flair for the ladies. Lieutenant Gambino continued: "You will be out on the streets of New York City wearing the NYPD Blues." The old choker always reminded me of the U.S. Marines' dress blues—the leatherneck look. And the ladies *loved* a man in uniform. "Bar owners will love to have you in or about their establishments," Gambino continued, "and the bad guys would love to give you a few bucks to look the other way." His message came through loud and clear.

It was maybe my fourth week at the academy when I was called into the commanding officer's office. I thought *Oh shit! What's the problem? Did they find out that my mother's uncles were West Side numbers men?* I *never* mentioned that on my paperwork. Joe the wop, Moo Cow, and others, including the Lancia family, were my mom's family. They ran with "Trigger" Burke and also the Corcorans. The name was an Irish name, but as I was to learn many years later, the real name was Corcorella, and when they migrated here at the turn of the century and the democratic club required firemen to be Irish or German, the two brothers became

"Irish." I had a cousin who was a police sergeant in the Bronx. We met on a few occasions. He was a Corcoran. I never told him the real deal. It didn't really matter.

As I entered the office, there were two men dressed in civilian clothes. (I called such men *suits*, but on the West Side they were referred to as *bulls* or *dicks*.) I was introduced by the commanding officer. A few weeks before I reported to the academy, I had received a call to come down to police headquarters at 100 Centre Street. At an office there, I was introduced to a detective who asked me if I would be interested in doing undercover work. I had said "Yes sir" like a good recruit and figured everyone got a similar call. I never heard another word about it, but I recognized one of the suits as the man I met at police headquarters. Now I knew it wasn't about my mother's family. I was told this would be my road to a gold shield, and in very short manner. I figured I'd give it a shot.

I was sent back to the class, and that weekend I was called at home and told to report to a location on Peck Slip. I was told not to forget my gun and shield. The whole weekend, my head was swirling. I hadn't even finished the academy. But I did recall a few officers in other companies who were in dress blues and had gold shields and were going through the academy.

I arrived bright and early at the location. I guess I appeared young at that time, because the desk sergeant gave me a hard time. He wanted to see my ID card; the shield was not enough. Anyway, he finally let me go on my merry way. Of course, as I learned over the years, NYPD shields are a hot commodity on the counterfeit market.

As I climbed each set of old stairs, I wondered what lay ahead. I was greeted—or should I say met—by an old lieutenant. His name is not important. "Hey kid, I hear you are quite familiar with the city, especially Manhattan," he said.

I explained that I had grown up in Hell's Kitchen and had sold papers all along the West Side. He dismissed me with a wave of the hand as he plopped down a file. All I could see was a part of a picture of me in the Department of Personnel folder from when I applied to the police department. Then he got up from his desk.

"First things first," he said. "Give me your gun, your shield, and ID card." I was starting to get the drift as he turned his back and locked them in a safe in the corner of the room.

He then sent me to lunch and told me to return in about two hours. When I returned, the office was full of activity. There were a number of men, mostly black and Hispanic, all in 1970s mod clothes: pimp hats, bell bottoms, and high-heeled shoes.

Hey, here I am in The Mod Squad, I thought. Not so. As I would find out later, looks can be deceiving. The lieutenant told me to go home. "You'll hear from us. You are now Delta 25. You call here each day. You will be told where to go for your assignments and told where your paycheck is. Never come back to this office unless you are directed by *me*."

I knew none of the men, and I never saw them again. My job was to be out in the field, and *never* to come to the office unless directed to be there. My paycheck was left at various banks in and around Wall Street. I would go and see the bank manager. He would then give me an envelope filled with cash for two weeks pay. We were paid every two weeks and never at the same bank.

I have promised never to reveal the details of what I was asked to do, and I will never violate that oath other than to say it involved surveillance. I wore civilian clothes, even to class, because I could get the call to undercover duty at any time. Over the years, I learned about great heroes who went undercover in the Black Panthers and FALN without spending even a day at the academy. When they finished their assignments, they did get the coveted detective's gold shield, as promised.

But what I was asked to do was of a different nature. I did some of it, and there were some things I refused to do, as they went against the principles by which I lived my own life. The lieutenant was not very pleased with me, and at times he threatened to withdraw the promise of the gold shield. He was barking up the wrong tree. At the time, I was not thinking so much about being a detective and what my weekly salary would be. My image of police work was pretty much focused on the picture of the sweating cop on the street coming to the aid of a civilian in trouble. In my mind, my office would be a radio car with emergency lights on the roof and a God-awful blaring siren to clear the streets for Al as he came to the rescue.

In January of 1971, the PBA called a job action, and my whole class was assigned to the street. I was assigned to Far Rockaway and was quickly on the street in freezing weather. We went on all the radio runs that the regular cops would have. All the patrolmen were in the sitting room, and there were many fistfights over the issue of whether or not they should continue striking.

We were doing twelve-hour tours, and on my second night, I was sent to do crowd control at a fire scene where someone had died. So that meant staying on the street with very few breaks. I thought my feet and hands would fall off. The strike lasted about one week, and the city survived, as did all of my graduating class.

Upon graduation, I was assigned to report to the Eighty-first Precinct in Brooklyn. I have to admit I was disappointed. I wanted a more glamorous, high-profile assignment—maybe something in Midtown Manhattan.

I had been in the 8-1 a couple of times, so I thought the precinct was pretty decent, if not glamorous. Before reporting, I called the 8-1, looking for some guidance about directions and when I should exactly report. The telephone switchboard cop laughed at me after I told him I was just assigned from the academy and hung up. I called back two times with the same response. At first I thought I had the wrong number. Well, with the next call, the response was, "Hey kid, who did you piss off? Okay, if it's daytime, follow the smoke; if it's nighttime, follow the flames. Welcome to the Hole in the Donut."

Chapter Five

LAST TOUR IN THE 8-1

. . . I did not seek blood

During the Williamsburg siege, I was assigned to the Eighty-first Precinct. It was my first assignment since graduating the academy, and while not glamorous, it suited my desire to be an active cop. I was sometimes partnered with Ronnie George, an academy classmate and, like me, a cop who wanted to stay busy, work hard, and make it home safely at night.

It was not unusual for a young, "piss-and-vinegar" cop to get paired up with an older "sour grapes" veteran who knew every trick in the book to avoid work. Some of those guys worked harder at avoiding work than they would have if they had just showed up and actually done the job. Getting teamed with a guy like that could put an early damper on a young cop's career. It took great determination to resist the cynicism and politicking of the older guys. So I was fortunate to be with a like-minded cop like Ronnie.

We stood out in the 8-1 because of our energy and our honesty. Ronnie and I made a bribery arrest of a bodega owner who was actually using his shop to deal great amounts of drugs. He told detectives stories about cops in the 8-1 willing to "look the other way in return for a six-pack or a carton of cigarettes." The precinct, in the days before the Knapp commission, had its share of "bad eggs"—detectives who had been demoted to patrolmen or were known to be under investigation.

One of the most bizarre incidents I ever witnessed involved one of those cops under suspicion. I was at a four-by-twelve roll call one day when a cab driver came into the precinct to report that he had been robbed. When the desk officer asked if he could give a description of the robber, the cabbie suddenly yelled out, "Him, that's him!" while pointing his finger at a cop on duty at the precinct switchboard.

All us guys in formation waiting to be turned out cracked up. *This cabbie must be nuts,* we thought. Well, we were wrong. The detective squad held a lineup, and sure enough, the cop was fingered by other cabbies that had been held up in Brooklyn not far from the 8-1. It turned out that the cop had a bad heroin habit and was sticking up cabs on his way to work every day while some cops looked the other way. He was an angel who fell all the way to the bottom; he lost his job and pension, and he even did some jail time.

That bodega drug dealer, who turned out to be quite a kingpin, could not believe it when Ronnie and I resisted his offers of booze, cigarettes, and, finally, cash—$5000—to let him go after we nabbed him for making a sale. That's when we collared the bodega owner and recovered several bags of heroin. He was stunned because it was not too long before, in 1972, that the Knapp commission, while investigating corruption in the NYPD, revealed to the world that throughout the department, there was a tolerance for being on the take that boiled like acid in the stomachs of honest cops.

Commanders at the highest levels believed that as much as 5 percent of the force was made up of outright crooks that were famously called "meat eaters." These were cops who actively sought opportunities to steal. They stole drugs, they extorted payoffs for protection, and they robbed from corpses.

The Knapp commission concluded that it was very common for a cop to be a "grass eater"—a cop who participated in petty corruption. Such a cop would accept a small bribe from a tow-truck operator for access to a highway breakdown or from a bar owner for the promise of keeping a closer eye on his place or turning a blind eye to after-hours activity.

Pimps, drug dealers, and unlicensed businessmen paid their "taxes" to the "grass eaters" and went about their business. For a young cop working in a precinct, there was tremendous pressure to become a "grass eater." Older, veteran cops, even training officers, taught the rookies what was expected of them regarding their cut of a Christmas present from a local businessman and which sergeants handled the distributions both up the ladder and down. The message was: "There's something here for you, kid, if you want it, and if you don't want it, that is your business, but keep your mouth shut."

That was life in the precincts before Knapp, and although we were still the best police department in the world, if you did not want to be on the take, then life was a little more complicated.

As for me, well, I locked up that bodega owner, and by the mid-'70s the message was out everywhere. We were a cleaner police force, and better off for it.

When we got him back to the precinct, the precinct's executive officer, Captain Arthur Duetsch—a legendary cop known as an honest boss who would look for good cops to promote, not just cops who had influential rabbis or other political influence—was on the scene. Even if the brass at headquarters wanted a cop's skin for one reason or the other, Artie would stand by the cop if he thought he was being treated unfairly. He was not afraid of anyone.

Artie was also known for a front-page news exploit when he stormed, guns blazing in both hands, a bank of telephone booths in Central Park where a psycho gunman had positioned himself and was shooting at anything that moved. Artie killed the guy.

He was the duty officer for the 14th Division that night, and he called Ronnie and me into his office and congratulated us and gave us an additional day off as a reward.

Later he called me back alone for a talk. He explained to me that for a cop of my dedication, the 8-1 assignment was a dead end. He confided that he was soon to be transferred to the Special Operations Division. He knew I wanted to go there, and he said he would not forget me.

The legendary cop kept his word. It was not long after that quiet meeting with him that I received a call at home. It was the desk lieutenant at the 8-1. "Hey kid, I don't know who you know, but you've been transferred to SOD," he said.

I certainly knew what he meant. The Special Operations Division was the parent command of the elite NYPD Emergency Service Unit. What I had thought about since I was a little boy was happening. I could hardly hold the phone steady in my hand.

The "Lou" was still talking, but I could not hear a word he was saying. I was so excited that my heart was thumping. I was smiling my ass off and crying at the same time.

He started shouting, "Do you hear me?"

"Yes sir," I shot back. "I'm transferred to SOD, yes sir. When do I report?"

"Well, champ, you have to do this one more tour . . . orders are not official until 12:01 tomorrow morning, so get your lazy ass in here."

"Thanks, Boss!" I said, and then I ran around the house, telling anyone who would listen.

When I arrived at the station house that afternoon, three of the other guys selected by Captain Duetsch were waiting for me outside.

"Hey Al, did ya hear? We're all out of here."

It was almost like being transferred out of the DMZ and into Saigon. One more shift. I couldn't believe it. During roll call, my mind drifted back to Manhattan's Hell's Kitchen, the place where I had grown up—a bucket of blood. I had two fond memories of growing up in Hell's Kitchen. One was that every Saturday I would go to Jack Dempsey's restaurant on Broadway and have lunch with him. My other was going to the Eighteenth Precinct station house on West Fifty-fourth Street. Its facade was made famous by all the old cop movies in the '40s and '50s. It was also the backdrop for the TV series *Naked City*. Little did anyone know that ESU Truck 18 was quartered in the rear of the station house. It was a classic open-model Mack truck painted deep green with gold leaf lettering reading "Police Emergency Service" on the sides and "NYPD" on both sides of the hood. It even had a bell and siren.

My uncle, Sergeant Bill Monahan, was assigned to the ESU behind the Eighteenth Precinct on West Fifty-fourth Street. I always got the royal tour. That's when the dream started. I wanted to grow up and become an E-Man. Every Sunday, the squad drilled. I was always there, watching in amazement as they practiced all their rescue techniques.

My daydream was ended by Sergeant James Lampeter. Lampeter was a WWII veteran. My generation of cops was very fortunate to work with these guys. They certainly were a "great generation." He was street hardened and had no ambition for higher rank, although I know he would have made an excellent boss.

"Hey Sheppard, read back the alarms," he called out to me.

He knew I had been off on my virtual tour through memory lane. I had forgotten to write the alarms on the rear page of my memo book. It was customary at that time that during roll call, the stolen vehicle teletype was called out. Officers were required to record the alarms in their memo books. The sergeant then snapped, "Sheppard, stand fast after roll call."

I thought, *Oh shit. I'm almost out of here, and now I'm gonna get a rip* [that's cop talk for charges]. The sergeant completed the inspection of the outgoing platoon. He posted them. And everyone was leaving for their sector cars or foot posts. I was scheduled to ride in Sector Charlie with Louie Barber.

I bet that because of the trouble I was in, I would be on a foot post, most likely on the far outskirts of the precinct. I waited in the muster room for what seemed like an hour. Actually, it was about fifteen minutes. Lampeter came strolling back. He put his arm over my shoulder. He said, "Listen kid, I've been on this job thirty years. Ten years ago, I made sergeant. Prior to that, I was in the trucks. I never had a big enough 'rabbi' to get me back to the ESU as a boss." In the NYPD, a rabbi is a higher-up willing to take someone under his or her wing, but I never wanted to play the "politics" necessary to get one.

"I know you will do fine," the veteran continued. "But you better pay attention to all the old hairbags and your training. If you think working here was dangerous, just wait and see."

"Hey Sergeant, I thought you were pissed at me," I said.

He smiled and said, "Shepp, you're a good cop, an honest cop, and full of piss and vinegar."

He talked about a night two years before when two cops were shot on Lexington Avenue and seriously wounded. I was his chauffeur that night—the boss's driver.

He recalled arriving on the scene, responding to reports of two officers down. I was anxious but cool as I sped to the address. It was a battle scene. Shots were being exchanged by the cops of the 8-1 and the perp, who was holed up in a house across the street. Both officers had been shot without provocation by a sniper. The gun smoke hung low in the hot, humid air. You could smell it blocks away. There was no command element at the scene.

That's the night I gained my respect for Sergeant Lampeter. With a hail of bullets flying over our heads, we both exited the patrol car from the driver's side and then crouched low behind the front fender while we took in the scene. Lampeter told me to reach inside the car and get him the public address microphone. He took the mike from me and shouted into it, "Cease fire; cease fire!"

The street fell immediately silent. With a loudspeaker, two words, and the courage to rush to the line of action, the sergeant had taken complete command in a matter of less than two minutes. The perp also stopped shooting, and the only real noise was the sound of approaching sirens—ESU units coming to our assistance.

Lampeter and I kind of half crawled, using the protection of parked cars, and he signaled to me to go to the front door of the perp's house. I made my way to the side and, again on the sergeant's signal, pounded on the door.

To the surprise of everyone involved in this incident, the door opened, and an elderly black man appeared in the doorway.

"I surrender; my name is George Washington," he said to me, and I quickly tossed and cuffed him while the other cops tried to use their nightsticks on him, although because of my being so short, I wound up getting most of the blows.

I ended up making the collar on the cop shooter. It was my first time on the front page of the *New York Post*. It was not to be my last.

In court the next morning, it was clear that George Washington was a deranged guy. He was lucky he did not kill one of those cops.

"Officer, how come this defendant is not in the hospital?" the judge said to me. He was an old-timer who loved cops and would not have been unhappy if we had blown away Mr. Washington.

I told him I just wanted to cuff the prick, and that is the truth. He shot two of my colleagues, but I did not seek blood. My job at that moment was to arrest him. Had he come to the door with a gun in his hand, the story would have had a different ending.

Back at the precinct after court, a long line of cops waited outside the captain's office while I was debriefed in the presence of my PBA delegate. Winks and nods from the delegate helped me correctly answer the captain's questions.

He said, "I can't believe you were there for the whole shootout and never fired a shot." I replied, telling him that Sergeant Lampeter had brought the situation under control and that with me being the smallest guy there, I had wanted to make the collar.

Leaving the captain's office, I was "honored" by my fellow cops with several blows to my head from their nightsticks. It was good-natured, but most of the guys would have rather seen me kill George Washington.

"I knew you had something special that night, and I know it now," Lampeter said to me. "Now go out and finish this last 8-1 tour, and make us all proud when you get to SOD."

Louie Barber was waiting for me in the RMP. Louie was known as "The Goat," but I never figured out why, and he would never say. He was a good cop—honest and active.

He leaned over and said, "So you're out of here. Good for you." I asked him why he stayed in the 8-1. "Travel, Al, travel." At the time, being a new kid on the block, I didn't understand this. Many cops lived outside the city. So if they were assigned to an outer borough like Brooklyn, it was easier to travel. There were no tolls, and not much traffic except for day tours—eight-by-fours. It made sense. Getting out of Manhattan was almost impossible, especially at rush hour. Louie rode a Harley Electra Glide, rain or shine, winter or summer. At that time, most cops "stopped" after the four-by-twelve shift. That meant going to a local gin mill and throwing down a few. I asked Louie why he always rode that Harley. "Good on gas, Al, good on gas," was his reply.

He was one of the original cops who left the city and moved the eighty or so miles to the "Original Cop Land," Nassau and Suffolk counties, both east of NYC, where homes were reasonable, there was hardly any crime, and the schools were good. Who would want their kids to go to school in the city? It would have to be a private school, and that cost a quarter of a cop's yearly salary.

That night seemed to fly by. We did job after job. The 14th Division radio in Brooklyn North was never silent—just the way I liked it. This was my last tour. I'd be reporting Monday to ESU Headquarters. The future looked bright. My boyhood dream had come true. I'd be entitled to wear the distinct patch of NYPD-ESU. I would also have Friday, Saturday, and Sunday off. The patrol chart in the 1970s never gave an officer a full weekend off.

It was 11:30, a half hour to go, when suddenly the 14th Division dispatcher came on the air: "In the 8-1 Precinct, report of a 10-30. Saratoga and Stone, a social club." A "social club" was nothing more than an unlicensed bar. They were prominent in poorer neighborhoods. A 10-30 was a robbery in progress. It was on the bordering sector. Eight-one Adam acknowledged the call. We advised that we would be backing up, as did Sector Boy. The club was in the middle of the block between Saratoga Avenue and Howard Avenue. I told Sector Adam we would come in from the opposite side down the wrong way on Stone, a one-way street that housed the local Black Panther Party headquarters.

As I turned the patrol car onto Stone Street, I put the high beams on. I also made sure everything was quiet at Black Panther headquarters. This might be a setup. Putting on the high beams ensured that the approaching cars and foot traffic would not be able to make out our patrol car. I could see Sector Adam pull just short of the location. There was a man in the street waving his arms. I gunned the accelerator. A large crowd was now exiting the club. Some had head wounds. Luckily, they were not shot, but pistol-whipped. The man was still shouting. "Them black motherfucker niggers ripped us off," he was screaming. He himself was a black man.

Suddenly a man motioned to me by cocking his head several times. I walked over to him. I recognized him as an officer from the adjoining Seventy-ninth Precinct, which bordered the 8-1 to the south. I acknowledged him without a word. He was lucky that the stickup team didn't search everyone. If they had, he would have been executed. It would not be the first time a cop was killed in a bar during a stickup.

He said, "Be careful. They're on foot, all drugged up, one with a .45 auto and the other with a sawed-off shotgun. The one with the large Afro and leather jacket has the shotgun. The shorter guy has the .45." I thanked him. He didn't have to offer the information. If he were known to have been in a social club it could mean his job. At the least it would mean an immediate suspension and most likely a thirty-day pay loss and a year's probation. He knew I wouldn't give him up. He was concerned for our safety. It was a different time in the NYPD. It was a time of brotherhood. The NYPD didn't allow its officers to frequent these types of establishments. I'd never give up another officer. That is, unless it was for corruption or brutality.

Sector Adam was taking the report. Louie and I started to canvass the area. I told Louie what the cop had told me. We put the description over the air. I cut the patrol car into Broadway where it intersected Saratoga Avenue. I drove a good six blocks down Broadway, then across Gates where it intersected with Saratoga. This was the direction they would be going unless they lived somewhere in between. But Gates Avenue was a subway stop, so I relied on my cop instinct.

In about four minutes, we spotted two male blacks crossing the darkened schoolyard. The streets were deserted because of the cold weather. I couldn't make out their clothing because of the darkness. I knew that it wasn't unusual for stickup teams to shed their outer garments to avoid being identified, but I thought they might not do this because of the cold. We made a decision to cut them off. This way we could foil any attempt for a clear escape route.

I let Louie out. He was going to make his way behind them. He used the parked cars on the opposite side of the street to cover his advance. I drove two blocks south to Monroe Street. Then I made a left onto Ralph Avenue, hoping my tire squealing turn didn't alert them. I parked the patrol car a half a block from the corner. I'd go the rest of the way on foot. As I exited, the wind picked up. I didn't realize how cold it had become. The cold air hitting my exposed face awoke all my senses. As I backed myself into the entrance of a closed store, I remembered to trust my survival instincts.

As I peered out cautiously, I could see that they were about three-quarters of the way down the block. I could also make out Louie darting back and forth in the street. He had now crossed over to the side they were walking on. He was crouching and moving like a deer. He was quite a cop.

As the two passed under the only working streetlight on the block, I could see them clearly. They fit the off-duty cop's description to a tee. My heart began to race as I slid my Smith & Wesson 9mm from its shoulder holster. This was my backup gun; the official .38 round-nose ammo would be no match for a shotgun and a .45 auto. My heart was now beating so hard I thought they could hear it. Sweat rolled down my face. They would be nearing the corner any minute now. I recalled the instructions given to me at the outdoor range: "Almost all police gun fights are at seven yards and last seven seconds, according to our stats. That's twenty-one feet—way too close for a mistake."

It was now or never. The element of surprise was always a benefit in combat, whether it was in the concrete jungles of "Bed Sty" or the jungles of Vietnam. Some call it an ambush, but it is always the surprise factor. I sprang like a cat out of the darkness, moving instantly into the police combat position with my 9mm aimed at their body masses. They would be no match for the copper-jacketed hollow points, not unless they were wearing bulletproof vests.

"Freeze, motherfuckers!" I shouted.

There was a brief moment of shock and disbelief on their faces. They went to turn, but Louie was right behind them, at the rear of a parked car not more than six feet away.

"Hands up, motherfuckers!" was Louie's order.

I knew at that point they had thought I was alone—a cop on foot patrol. I would have been no match by myself. And if they hadn't wanted a confrontation, I'd have had to chase them on foot. They were never expecting another officer right behind them. Boy was he a great street cop. He may have been a guy who cared most about being as close to home as possible, and maybe he was not the most ambitious cop I ever worked with, but he was a calm, cool, collected, and highly professional cop. He taught me a lot about police work that night.

We slowly closed in on them, watching every move. We knew now that they were the perps, both armed and dangerous. We quickly overtook them, throwing them in a spread-eagle position up against the parked car. Louis reholstered his service revolver. I stood back, maintaining cover. I warned Louie that the little guy had the .45 and told him it should be in his waistband. Sure enough, it still had blood on it from where he had pistol-whipped one of the patrons.

Louie put the .45 down on the sidewalk and, without looking down, used his foot to slide it back to me. The other perp had the sawed-off shotgun. It was secured by a sling made of clothesline hanging from his shoulder. All he would need to do would be pull his jacket back and level the weapon. It would only take a second for him to get off a round. By this time, several backup squad cars were on the scene. The patrol sergeant told us to go back to the station house and start the paperwork. Sector Adam would take the perps back to the social club for a positive ID. Even though there was no doubt as to who they were, procedure had to be followed.

When we got back to the station house, Louie told me he would take the collar. He said, "I know you're out of here." I looked up at the large, black, official NYPD clock hanging over the desk officer's location. I replied by saying, "Not yet, Louie. It's 11:57. Three more minutes to go." We both laughed. As I packed my locker, I thought back to all the sorrow I had witnessed here in the 8-1. In the past few years, I had seen a lot of harm inflicted by people on one another: homicides, rapes, assaults of every kind, dead babies, and children who had no hope for the future. I found out just how cheap life was on the streets of America's ghettos. And the shame of it all was that there were many fine people living in this ghetto. I grew to know many of them. I was treated as family and invited to weddings, christenings, and family parties. They say you can choose your friends but not your family. I know that the majority of the people did not choose to be there, but they were left with no choice.

But now I was going somewhere where I could help people by doing good. This meant dealing with people who would be happy to see the police responding. We would be there to save lives. I was no longer forced to serve as a member of an army of occupation for the corrupt political machines whose justice was meted out to the poor and less fortunate. Remember, "Cops don't make the laws; they only enforce them."

That evening, "stopping off" was something special. All in all, Captain Duetsch had taken care of six of his guys by arranging to get us out of the dead-end 8-1 and into assignments we wanted. Some wanted to be detectives; others wanted spots that would suit their travel needs.

Most of the guys in the saloon that night agreed with my desire to go to SOD. Some thought it was nuts. "Why climb bridges to bring down some psycho who wants to kill himself anyway?" some opined. Others thought of E-Men as "firemen with guns." I thought those guys were a little jealous of my good fortune.

Usually, the only way to get into ESU was to volunteer as a summer fill-in, and after a few summers passed, you might get the nod for a permanent spot. Another way was to have a rabbi. I think I got in because my hard work was noticed by an honest cop who sincerely wanted the best for the department.

Together with the retelling of how Louie and I took down the two desperadoes, it was a raucous but good-natured night. Needless to say, I went home burning with energy and very much looking forward to the weekend passing so that I could report to SOD as E-Man Al Sheppard.

I never fully discussed my transfer with my family. They thought police work was dangerous enough. They wondered why someone would put himself in danger on a regular basis for the same pay earned by a cop riding a desk. They had a point, and I wish I had taken more time to explain my feelings to them. Perhaps my family life would have been a little less stressful had I done so. But when you're looking back, it is easy to know what you should have done.

Chapter Six

ESU TRAINING

... You will live and die with your decisions

It is no secret (because I tell everyone I know) that one of the greatest days in my life was the day I reported for training as a member of the Emergency Service Unit. The Special Operations Division is world-renowned for its training methods and the thoroughness with which it instills the skill and knowledge necessary into otherwise competent but not "special" cops.

Don't get me wrong; I have all the respect in the world for the guy or gal who works every day in any NYPD job. Some of them are among the best cops in the world, whether they patrol a raw, inner-city neighborhood or teach rookies at the police academy.

There are cops who have spent twenty years walking beats who I would trust with my life in a second. They have learned more about human nature, the science of criminology, and the means of survival than most of us will ever know. Many of those cops are happy to serve in their small roles, not seeking the spotlight and not in need of more adrenaline than they get on their regular rounds, and they prove themselves a hundred times a day.

New York's detectives are the standard-bearers for detectives everywhere. They are smart, streetwise, and wise in other ways. They are famous for their dogged pursuit of the bad guy. I could not have been prouder when I was a detective in the Major Case Squad.

The main objective of the NYPD ESU is to rescue and render emergency service to the people of the city of New York. But it is most especially to the members of the NYPD.

Every ESU unit is set up in exactly the same way so an officer going from one unit to another can swing right into operation. In my day, there were ten emergency service squads in the city, not including special units—such as the bomb squad, which had its own bomb and explosive removal trucks, the Air Bag Unit, which was deployed to high-rise fires and jumper calls with its giant pillow that allowed a jumper to walk away practically unscathed, and the Building Collapse Unit.

There are also trucks equipped with massive lights that can turn night into day at a crime scene, and there are also specialized command and communications units.

To be considered for ESU, a cop must have at least five years of service. Once selected, candidates attend specialized training schools before being sent to a unit where on-the-job training takes place. An ESU officer is a SWAT team member, an EMT certified by the State of New York, a scuba diver, and an expert on the ways in which buildings and bridges are constructed. Today ESU officers are even trained in pararescue so that they can drop from helicopters to save drowning people in the Atlantic Ocean off of Coney Island or boaters trapped in New York Bay. I probably would have gone for that if we'd had such a service then.

The first day I reported for weapons training at the police firing range at Rodman's Neck in the Bronx, I understood what made the men of ESU different. They were not better than any other cop, but they were *different* in a very real way.

As is the case in military training with the Special Operations Units, such as Marine Force Recon; my old outfit, the Army Airborne; or the legendary Navy SEALS, when a cop is assigned to ESU training, he is considered to be a rookie. It does not matter how many arrests he has made, how many miles he has driven with lights and sirens screaming, how many cats he has rescued from trees, or how many lost children he has returned to their parents. Rank and time on the job is put aside for the duration of training. There is no rank when one is admitted to the ESU Specialized Training School (STS) within the ranks of the Special Operations Division, of which ESU is a unit.

The ESU rookie had to become an "expert" in a variety of tasks.

Number one is qualifying as an expert in special weapons and tactics, or SWAT, as it is commonly known everywhere except in New York City. We did not need the fancy acronym to advertise our presence.

The firing range is located on the Bronx mainland, across the small bay from City Island. Here an ESU trainee is required to qualify on a variety of weapons, under every adverse condition. This means snow, wind, rain, subzero wind chills, and stifling summer heat. Day and night, the training and qualifying are conducted to simulate the way the situation would be encountered in the real world. There is a simulated "combat town" in which hostage recovery is taught because ESU is responsible for the safe recovery of hostages. If the decision is made to "storm" a location, it is ESU that does the assault.

During my career, I worked hand in hand with the one and only Captain Frank Bolz on many hostage jobs. Frank was the innovator of the NYPD Hostage Negotiation Team, which was organized right after the terror attack at the 1972 Olympics in Munich, Germany, where Israeli athletes were murdered by units of the Black September terror group. During these years, Frank Bolz ran the Hostage Negotiation Team. We are all proud to say we never lost a hostage.

ESU is designated as the assault team when negotiations fail and innocent lives hang in the balance. The negotiators, all from precinct detective squads at that time, were "talking heads." It was their job to try to make a personal association with the hostage taker, but from a safe distance. When they hit a dead end, it was ESU that was first in the door.

Some extractions were done covertly by fooling the hostage taker with a series of ploys to get his attention away from the hostage or from the area in which he was holding the hostage. As a member of ESU, you could be the entry team; this meant you would make forcible entries into locations. Or you could be on the assault team; this meant you were going through the door.

Innocent lives would be your responsibility. Once inside the location, the teams were responsible for the safe removal of the hostage. This meant properly identifying the innocent person and properly identifying the hostage taker. This would not work without good intelligence gathering—a process that started with the precinct's initial response.

There are several methods and pieces of equipment used for this process, and ESU members are trained on all of them. I will not divulge some of the secret methods of intel gathering, but rest assured that the NYPD is equipped with the latest high-tech equipment and knows how to use it.

Without this ongoing intel, it would be a difficult task to make the proper ID of the innocent victim and the hostage taker. Many times the hostage taker will exchange clothes with a victim and try to conceal himself among the hostages.

In our training, we would play out scenarios over and over again. For example, we would practice taking care of a bank robbery or stickup gone bad. The hostage situation is likely the most difficult assignment in ESU. This is where innocent lives hang in the balance entirely on your decisions.

Sometimes, despite all the training, things could go terribly wrong. Just because an ESU officer is highly trained and properly equipped does not mean he or she is safe from injury or death. It is driven into trainees that ESU must play by the rules; the perps cannot survive if they play by the rules. There have been ESU officers killed and wounded because of the restraints placed on the division. In my opinion, one in particular was the senseless death of hero ESU officer Joe McCormick, which troubles me to this day.

I feel that when people shoot at another person, cop or civilian, they have made their decision. They have shown a willingness to throw away their own lives for whatever reason brought them to that point. It's an outlaw mentality, and cops learn to expect it and deal with it. McCormick was ready for it, but he was handcuffed by politics.

Life on the street is not a game. Death is a very real possibility. It was never truer than on September 29, 1983, on Moffat Avenue in the Bronx in the Forty-fifth Precinct. ESU's Joe McCormick and his partner, Dave Schultheis, responded to a report of a male who had barricaded himself in his home but was exiting every few minutes to fire a shotgun at whatever target was available. He was, in effect, holding the entire neighborhood hostage. People were afraid to move. Traffic was shut down for blocks around. The precinct cops who first responded gave him many chances to throw down the gun and surrender before someone was seriously hurt. He had responded by firing at them.

They could have easily returned his fire and no doubt brought him down, but the SOD commander at the scene had given a clear order: Do not return fire unless civilians are directly at risk, and no tear gas. The commander believed he had the situation contained and was awaiting the Hostage Negotiation Team to talk the shooter down. In New York, that is often the case. NYPD does not, as a matter of policy, operate as if it patrols the Wild West. Oftentimes, the restraint we showed was admirable, even though it could be deadly.

When Joe arrived, he took cover behind a large tree in the man's yard, giving the first responders a chance to back out to safety. As soon as he saw Joe going for position, the perp came out on his porch and fired a blast in Joe's direction. The round struck the tree and then entered Joe on the exposed side of his heavy vest.

It was a freak shot—you could say it was bad luck—but it never should have gotten to that point. The result was a heroic ESU officer killed in the line of duty. On seeing McCormick hit, Schultheis opened fire and killed the perp with one shot.

I repeat my opinion: if an armed person who has had the opportunity to put down his weapon refuses to surrender, he has had his opportunity. There is no reason that an officer should needlessly be placed in harm's way. This is also true for the public we protect. I don't want to be a Monday morning quarterback, but if I were calling the plays on that tragic day, the only fatality would have been the perp. It is better to be judged by twelve than carried by six.

There is no better trained special weapons and tactics unit in the entire country than the NYPD ESU. It's a matter of fact. The weapons restraint is unsurpassed by any other organization. The range instructors are, in my opinion, the best in the entire U.S. police service. Many are former police officers that have been involved in combat situations. There is no better teacher than reality; the second best is someone who survived and lived to talk about it.

The ESU trainee is expected to qualify with all the weapons in the ESU arsenal, which include sniper rifles, machine guns, automatic handguns, and a number of projectiles used in barricade situations and other tactical assignments. They could range from "flash bang" grenades to tear gas projectiles. The ESU officer, once qualified in the special weapons course, must continue to requalify every several weeks, no matter what the weather conditions or the season. In addition, the ESU officer is trained in the proper identification of explosive devices and the proper ways to make safe any device.

It is also the ESU's responsibility to remove explosives via special explosive removal vehicles. ESU works hand and glove with the NYPD Bomb Squad. The majority of detectives in the bomb squad are former ESU officers. Whenever a suspected explosive is found, ESU is called. It is the responsibility of the ESU to decide if the bomb squad should also respond.

I recall being on several jobs where we found pipe bombs, dynamite, and other explosives. One in particular was in Pennsylvania Station. The bombs were placed in lockers. Several went off. These were designed to maim innocent persons. Fortunately, no one died that day. They were made from propane bottles, blasting caps, and several boxes of nails. This would inflict severe injury to anyone in the area. I was able to render one inoperative. It appeared that it was defective.

The training is never over when one becomes a member of the NYPD ESU. It is a constant program. After time and training as a member of ESU, you think and act as part of a unit. It is a true team with a tradition equal to the elite military units of the present and the past.

All ESU officers are SCUBA qualified. This means they can dive in all the waterways, lakes, and rivers in and around NYC. Don't forget that Manhattan is an island. New York City is surrounded by water: the Hudson River, the East River, Long Island Sound, New York Bay, and even the Atlantic Ocean. Some assignments are water rescue situations. A small, private aircraft might ditch in the Hudson River, or a giant 747 might go off the runway at JFK and into the Atlantic.

New York is a diverse place, and its emergencies reflect that diversity. People fall from walkways into the river or jump from bridges or drive their cars, not always by accident, off of piers and into the river. Every year, many people owe their lives to ESU officers who braved the currents of the dangerous waters that surround the city of New York. They rescue children who fell through the ice, and sometimes they rescue pets that are trapped on chunks of ice floating toward the ocean.

Every ESU officer is required to be an EMT licensed by New York State. Some ESU officers are now paramedics. Every officer is qualified to rappel out of helicopters and off of fixed objects, such as buildings and difficult terrain. I'm proud to say I was the first ESU officer to rappel out of a helicopter in 1977. Of course, I had experience at it in 'Nam.

It is also the responsibility for ESU to remove jumpers. This could take place on a building, a bridge, or even a two-hundred-foot construction crane. I've been on all of them—many times.

Every year, hundreds of people are rescued by the members of ESU. The ESU has saved people from mangled automobile wrecks, trapped in machinery, trapped under subway trains, caught in elevators, trapped by cave-ins at construction sites, and trapped in fires or building collapses.

In my career, I have worked all of these situations. Most were successful rescues. I owe it all to my training. The training in ESU has allowed me to save many lives. But it has also allowed me to save my own life. All the above rescue scenarios are practiced over and over again at the Specialized Training School and at the various ESU squads throughout the city.

But simulation training is simulation. Jumping off the platform at airborne school was nothing like jumping from a plane the first time I did it. Nothing in the police academy was anything like the real streets, not even the simulated combat course at the pistol range. In my opinion,

ESU cops do not learn the job until they get out on the street and do it.

That seems to be a simple proposition: on-the-job training—it's done in a lot of professions, but not when lives hang in the balance. That is why new ESU officers, after graduation and assignment to a squad, are teamed up with a veteran ESU officer. This is the training that is most valuable. They learn that there is always another avenue by which to accomplish a rescue. No two are ever alike. Veterans tell the rookie never to give up; there is always another option.

The ESU officer must be knowledgeable and proficient in his job, never forgetting that seconds matter. It could be the difference between life and death. As a member of ESU you must be able to adapt to any situation in seconds. There is no room for panic. You must think on your feet and think like an Einstein. There is no margin for error when a life is at stake. You will live or die because of your decisions; you will take them home with you at night, and you will replay them over and over again in your mind. If you make the right call, you will think you are lucky. Next time, you might make the wrong call, and someone might die, maybe even a cop.

I have no doubt that without the training I received in ESU Specialized Training School and the heavy weapons training, I wouldn't be here to write this memoir. I would be six feet under; my picture hanging on a wall of honor somewhere as another NYPD Fallen Angel. But ESU cops volunteer to put their asses on the line, and one reason they do it is that they know they will receive the best training available and get to work side by side with the best teachers in the world of law enforcement. It raises the odds, gives you a better chance to make it home at night, and allows you to be able to retire and have some life with your family.

After specialized rescue training at Floyd Bennett Field, I was sent to Truck 4 in the Bronx, a rookie once more. It was a busy truck which actually covered the better parts of the Bronx. We spent a lot of time backing up Truck 3, which included in its patrol area Fort Apache in the South Bronx and all the other neighborhoods which, at that time, had sunk to new lows of crime and poverty—those two partners in the destruction of cities.

The first day I rang the bell on the quarters door, a stocky guy opened it.

"I'm Al Sheppard, reporting for duty," I said.

"I know who you are, and we know all about you; come on in," the cop said.

I was reminded of the NYPD grapevine—the underground communications network that never sleeps and never stops delivering rumor, innuendo, and, on some rare occasions, truth to the cops all over the city.

I carried my gear up to the second floor, which was over the garage where the trucks were parked, and asked a sergeant where my locker was.

"Kid, you passed your locker on the way up. It's in the hallway," he said. Well, I got it. I was the rookie again, and again I was going through a rite of passage just to earn the right to wear the ESU patch on my sleeve.

To my surprise (because I thought I was a hotshot cop, having made a collar that got me on the front page of the *Post* and having survived several shootouts in the 8-1), I was assigned as the ERM, the emergency records and management guy; in other words, I was the gofer, chief cook, and bottle washer—a useless rookie who couldn't find his dick when he needed to piss. The only time I would get into the action was when Adam or Boy trucks would call for the big truck—the War Wagon. That would mean that the shit had hit the fan somewhere.

When the War Wagon rolled, a patrolman would drive, a sergeant would be a passenger, and the ERM would sit in the back of the walk-in truck, bouncing all over the place until arriving at the job.

Once at the scene, I would still not get into the action. My job would be to pass out the heavy weapons and vests and other equipment to the "real" E-Men and then take responsibility for the security of the truck and its remaining gear.

After a few months of this initiation ritual, Detective Jack Shea, a legendary E-Man, agreed to take me under his wing and field train me. We patrolled in one of the smaller trucks, although it was still loaded with all kinds of unimaginable equipment.

Shea was a super cop. He was awarded the detective's gold shield for his excellent performance in his particular assignment, not for his sleuthing ability, although he would have been great at that also.

Truck 4 had some other characters, like Sergeant Mike Derby, who looked and acted like a marine drill instructor. He was a winner of the NYPD Medal of Honor.

Another sergeant—we called him The Greek—had survived being stabbed by a psycho. He too was a recipient of the Medal of Honor.

A third sergeant, named Jimmy Hollywood, was a typical Irish cop with a joke always at the ready.

My first ESU rescue job came while I was working with Shea. A poor soul had fallen under a train. We were sent to rescue him or remove what was left of him. We could not be sure until we got there. I was pumped up when, just as we were finishing our equipment checks, the citywide dispatcher called out over the radio, "Adam 4, Boy 4, man under, Fordham and Jerome."

We were first out of the garage. Jack, because he knew the neighborhood better than I, was driving, lights flashing and siren screaming. Boy 4 followed us, and as we started down the block, I caught a glimpse of the War Wagon, Truck 4, passing through the garage entrance.

At the scene, Jack hit the emergency brake, and as he jumped out of the cab, he yelled to me to bring the portable lights. He was already anticipating the scene we were heading into. He knew we would need our powerful portable light kits to illuminate the area under the train, which was on an elevated track at that point in the line.

We made our way through a gathering, curious crowd until we saw a transit authority cop waving his flashlight in the direction he wanted us to go.

Standing on the platform next to the train, Shea asked the transit authority cop to confirm that the power was off. We did not want to get electrocuted while going under the train to rescue this guy. The transit authority cop used his radio and got back a confirmation.

Jack stepped in between two cars and took a quick look below the train. He came back to me, picked up a body bag that he had carried up there and left on the floor, and handed it to me.

By this time Boy 4 was on the platform with us and Truck 4 was pulling in down below.

Shea threw the body bag to me and reminded me to put on my big work gloves. "He's all yours, kid. I'll come down right after you," the veteran said.

As I slid myself down to the track bed, I could smell burned flesh and clothing. The victim was wrapped around one of the big steel wheels. He was kind of bent in half, and his face was looking right at me as I maneuvered as close to him as I could get.

Thirty years later, I am still haunted by his stare. The electric shock had blown out his eyes, and there were just two empty holes in his head.

Mangled bodies, unless they were children, never really bothered me, but that stare was haunting. And the smell really got to me. You never forget the odor of burned human flesh.

I was fixated on this horrible sight and not doing my job. Shea slid in beside me, on his back. He brought me back to reality by saying, "This will take a while."

I had to put out of my mind the fact that some twenty minutes ago, this was a living human being. Now my job was to remove his remains and allow the trains to resume running.

In those years before more modern rescue tools, this kind of job was bull work. E-Man Ronnie Kind stuck his head down and asked us what we needed.

Shea asked for the ten-ton train jack and wooden chocks.

"Never put metal to metal," Shea reminded me. The wooden blocks, placed between the jack and the train, would prevent the jack from slipping. Here we were, in this bizarre situation, and Jack Shea was instructing me, not forgetting his job as a field trainer.

He told me to open the body bag and slide it under the body as he slowly lifted the train.

I learned that night that trains could be jacked up because they actually float on sets of wheels called trucks; they are not actually attached to the wheels that are on the tracks. Only its massive weight keeps it in place.

Per Shea's instructions, I pulled at the body until I felt some slack. He kept working the jack, and inch by inch, as the train car rose, I worked the body free. When I gave one hard tug, the remains broke completely free of the wheel and landed on top of Shea and me. We were covered in remains: intestines, blood, veins, and all kinds of gore that not long ago was a functioning human being.

Overcoming our disgust, we pulled the body clear and got it into the body bag. Boy 4 lowered a line, and we raised the full bag to the platform. The traffic authority cop tied a 9-5 tag—a dead-on-arrival (DOA) identification tag—to his big toe and noticed that the victim's right leg was missing.

Boy 4 was ordered to walk the tracks after the train pulled out to see if they could locate the leg. For us the job was over; it had taken about one hour, and as we pulled away, we heard the train pulling out of the station.

Back at quarters, Shea and I showered, changed clothes, and then sat down at the ever present gray table for a cup of coffee.

We heard Boy 4 pulling into the garage downstairs, and Ronnie King, in that Jimmy Cagney voice of his, quickly began telling us that they never found the leg.

"It must have fallen through the tracks onto a bus or truck, or maybe the rats ate it," he said.

Sadly, there would be many more body parts to come.

Chapter Seven

THE CALLS

. . . It was just another day

One rescue of a Con Edison worker still gives me goose bumps when I think about it. Gary Gorman and I were working an eight-by-four tour in Truck 1, which was known as the Hollywood Truck because it covered the glamorous areas of Manhattan and got many high-profile jobs. Day tours in Truck 1 were always busy, and you had plenty of media attention.

We had a very busy morning this one particular day. Then, just after lunch, we were dispatched by citywide radio to "an injured Con Ed worker . . . corner of Grand St. and Broadway." That is downtown Manhattan.

On arrival, we found the injured worker ten feet down in a manhole. He had been struck by a car that ran into the Con Ed work barriers. As I looked into the manhole, I could see his prone figure. He was surrounded by high-voltage electrical wires that were dancing just a foot above his head. Sparks were flying everywhere. With each explosion of sparks I was able to see the worker was bleeding heavily from a head wound. Here again, training and experience came into play. Instinctively, Gary and I realized time was of the essence. We had to get to him to stop the bleeding as quickly as possible. We did not discuss this; we just knew it. It was also obvious that he had suffered additional injuries. It appeared that one of his legs was broken by the way it lay mangled in the four-inch-deep water and muck at the bottom of the hole. I was amazed that he hadn't been electrocuted when he was knocked backwards into the manhole. He had to fall in the path of the high-voltage cables, which were dancing like electric snakes.

The precinct cops were dealing with the reckless driver who caused the accident and were maintaining traffic and crowd control. As fast as we had to move, we also knew we had to be cautious if we were to save his life. What good would two dead cops be to anyone? EMS was on scene, but they would not enter the manhole. That was our job. As we prepared, one of the victim's coworkers told us the victim was set to retire at the end of the week after thirty years of service with Con Edison.

I put on our heavy-duty, insulated, rubber ESU electrical gloves. Normally we used them to secure live wires on jobs when electrical poles were down and any other time we had overhead wires down. They were also needed when we had to deal with other hazardous electrical situations in which electrocution was a possibility.

With the ungainly gloves firmly on my hands, I started down the ladder, trying to avoid the five-inch-thick cables as they shot showers of sparks in every direction. I knew that with one wrong move, I would be toast, literally. The gloves allowed me to be able to push the live cables aside, avoiding contact as I made my descent into the dark pit. After a long descent, I finally reached the victim. He was bleeding badly from a serious head wound. I had to control the bleeding before I did anything else.

I called up to Gary to lower the trauma kit. "Slowly," I repeated as Gary lowered it to the bottom, inch by inch. The victim was barely conscious. We did not speak. When I got down there, it appeared to me that he had suffered two broken legs. This was going to be a nightmare.

I was able to control the bleeding of the head wound using six four-by-four compression dressings and one roll of bandage. I'd need splints for his leg injuries. There wasn't much room to work, and we were in several inches of murky water. This was hell on earth; it was dark, it was smelly from burned wires and insulation, there was a suffering victim, and I could hardly see. It would be impossible for the victim to climb out of this potential tomb. He'd have to be raised up manually.

Normally we would use a Stokes basket. But in this case that would be impossible, because a Stokes is made of metal and is lined with chicken wire. One contact between the Stokes and the cables would be disastrous. We'd all fry in that hole. Our only alternative would be a wooden backboard normally used to secure vehicle accident victims. By using one of these, we could place a cervical collar on the victim, immobilizing the neck and spinal column.

This was our only choice. This was going to be a tough extrication. One wrong move and we'd be goners. In order for Gary to lower the backboard, I would have to make a space by securing the electrical cables. They were still arcing and showering us with sparks every few minutes.

Gary dropped a work line of one-inch manila rope. Normally it was used in high-angle rescues. That was our work rope, which was never to be used to raise or lower a victim, but we'd used it to secure downed signs and to remove tree limbs as we cut them off a vehicle or house. Gary cut the line into four-foot lengths. Using these, I was able to secure the electrical cables to the metal conduits that ran along the wall, making sure the exposed ends were nowhere near the metal to complete a circuit.

Once I secured the cables, Gary was able to lower the backboard. But I needed help securing the victim to the board, so Gary had to join us in that hell that was the manhole. We barely had room to lay the board flat. Actually, we had to prop it up on an angle. Our victim was obviously in a tremendous amount of pain. My heart went out to him. Having myself been injured many times, I was no stranger to pain. We splinted both legs, and then we secured him with rope to the backboard.

I knew his ascent to daylight would be painful, but I hoped it would take only a couple of minutes. There was no other choice. As Gary climbed back to the street, he accidentally brushed against one of the cables. The result was another shower of sparks raining down on the victim and me. Once at the top, he started to pull the victim up. I carefully followed close behind, keeping the foot of the backboard from coming in contact with the cables. We finally made it to the top. Fresh air—wow, it was great to feel the sun on my face and to know we had saved another life.

Sometimes the calls were out of the ordinary, such as, for example, one we received on a quiet afternoon on June 24, 1975, around 2:00 p.m. or so. I was sitting on my ass in the NYPD's central repair shop in Queens. It is a cavernous place; more like an airplane hangar than an auto repair garage. A little earlier, my partner and I had been checking out Adam 4 in preparing to bring our particular brand of police service to the citizens of the Bronx when, during a routine check, we found the emergency roof lights were not working properly. They would spin a few times, freeze, spin again, freeze for a long period, spin a moment or two, and then freeze. We never liked taking out a unit that was not 100 percent up to par. Those lights made it possible to negotiate traffic on the way to an emergency. If we got stalled in traffic, we were not doing our job. If we had an accident on the way because a civilian driver did not see us coming, well, that would cost the city some moola. So, we asked permission to bring Adam 4 in to the repair unit. I figured it just needed a signal box—a small box that controlled the electric siren and all the emergency lights that were distributed around the truck. I could have easily repaired it myself if I'd had the part.

E-Men are jacks-of-all-trades. We're auto mechanics, electricians, steeplejacks, painters, typists, and also great complainers.

The citywide radio was fairly quiet. The Bronx was burning that year, but on that day, the Truck 4 units were not yet on the firing line. So we received permission from our supervisor, after I told him it would be quick, and we headed for the repair shop.

The enormous shop was a one-stop shopping mall for any problem that could befall an NYPD vehicle. It was filled with bays in which bodywork was done on mangled police cars. The civilians who worked there were pretty good mechanics. They did routine tune-ups and complicated repairs, and they were better paid than patrol cops. They were also enormous pains in the ass. They had the worst attitudes. If you brought your patrol car in and said the headlights needed adjustment, only after you filled out the proper paperwork would they adjust the headlights. Now suppose that while they were adjusting the headlights, one of the lights blew out. Believe me—and any of those who ever went there would agree—they would totally ignore the blown light unless you said something, and then you would have to fill out another form before they would touch it.

In a police department that prided itself on quick thinking, innovation, and teamwork, the repair unit stood out as a place to avoid at all costs. Those guys were not typical of most civilians we worked with, who were quick to help you with a problem. All had to follow the rules, and I guess they felt they were not treated with the same level of respect that the uniformed force received, although they usually made more money and they could be fairly certain they would return to their loved ones when their shift was over. In the repair shop, you had to dot the Is and cross the Ts and kiss the asses of a bunch of pompous pricks who made a good living doing what most teenage car freaks could do better and would be happy to do for free.

After I filled out the form saying the lights were not working and suggested it might be the fault of the signal box, the mechanic—a middle-aged guy who apparently managed to perform all kinds of repairs without getting his hands dirty—farted around for about an hour, took a coffee break, and finally proclaimed we needed a new signal box. We were at his mercy; we needed those lights; we loved those lights. I would always sneak a peek at them as we barreled along through an underpass or tunnel, and I totally loved the way they lit up a city street, reflecting off the windows and wet pavement. It was the Hollywood screenwriter in me that would imagine it looked like a movie set.

So, with lights and siren in working order, we reported to citywide that we were back in service, and we headed for the Triborough Bridge. We were about a mile or so from the bridge entrance ramp when the unusually quiet citywide radio came alive. "All ESU units in Queens," it stated, and that got our attention right away even though we were assigned to and headed for the Bronx. When a message began that way, it got everyone's attention. "Report of a commercial airliner down in the vicinity of Kennedy Airport," citywide continued, and then there was silence as Emergency Service Units all over the city absorbed the call.

This was a big one. All Special Operations Division units would be dispatched to a plane crash: E-Men from around the city, highway patrol, crime scene units, medical services, photo units, and probably some bomb squad guys also. The Port Authority cops—whose jurisdiction includes the area's three major airports, two major bridges, and a subway system—would also be on the scene. The FBI would send a team or two; the National Transportation and Safety Board would respond; the New York Fire Department would, of course, rush to the scene; and the Port Authority firefighting units would respond as well. Ambulances from the city's emergency medical service would join private hospital units, and the media would roll out its live trucks and every available photographer and reporter. Gary and I wanted Adam 4 to be there also. The entrance to the Van Wyck Expressway was about half a mile in front of us on the way to the bridge. That would give us a direct run to JFK Airport.

The citywide radio again began broadcasting. "We're receiving numerous 911 calls, commercial airliner down on Rockaway Parkway. This is confirmed by precinct units on scene."

I gunned the engine and Gary grabbed the mike. The radio was now buzzing with reports of units on the way to the scene, the chauffeurs for all the top brass were reporting in, and the police commissioner himself reported an ETA of twenty minutes. Gary joined in. "Citywide, Adam 4 is in the area. We are responding."

"10-4, Adam 4," replied the dispatcher, who may have wondered why we were in the area, but being the pro he was, he did not hesitate to log us in.

Our supervisor also heard our response and told citywide, "ESU supervisor, read direct." We were on our way. All of a sudden I could care less about the asshole mechanic; the lights and siren were wailing to perfection, and traveling at highway speed in excess of eighty miles per hour would put us on the scene in a matter of minutes.

My heart began to race. This was like a dustoff into a hot 'Nam landing zone with eight or nine gunships going in under fire. I saw a Chinook—a twin-rotor chopper—go down under small arms fire at Khe Sahn. It totally lost its hydraulics. It was sickening to see the valiant bird twisting and turning while trying to stay aloft. When it impacted, it burst into flame. Some of the 1ˢᵗ Cavalry troopers aboard got out, but even they were engulfed in flame. I wondered now if this crash would have survivors.

The rush was indescribable. In the ESU, we always joked about the "Big Job." John & Al's Williamsburg siege was a Big Job. This would be on the list as one of the Big Jobs. Until 9/11, there were many Big Jobs. But the World Trade Center attack created a new base of measurement for a Big Job. It was the ultimate Big Job, and I hope it is never exceeded.

Aircraft rescue is a part of ESU training. As we approached, I ran through some scenarios in my mind, but most of our practice had to do with hostage rescue, not crashes. We were taught how to enter aircraft from different doors and loading areas and how to target and fire once inside the cabin. I doubted that we would have an intact aircraft to work with this afternoon.

The Van Wyck was understandably gridlocked. We approached along the grass bank along the highway until we were able to roll into an area of carnage. There was no rescue work to be done here. It struck me as a battlefield with dead and dying everywhere. It appeared to me that there could be no survivors. Dozens of bodies were strewn about like rag dolls waiting for a little girl to retrieve them after a day of play. Some appeared to be asleep. Some were burned beyond recognition. There were decapitated bodies still strapped in their chairs.

Despite the sirens announcing the arrival of dozens of emergency units and the screams of passersby who had rushed to help at the scene, in my mind, it was eerily quiet, like a battlefield the morning after. Within minutes, units were on the scene from the fire department, police department, and EMS. Then a very strange thing happened; I had a thought of the movie *Zulu* starring Michael Caine, in which hordes of local residents descend on the scene of destruction following a battle, hell-bent on looting the dead. They were not there to render help. No, they were there to plunder and rape the victims. There were people crawling like roaches around the wrecked plane, the decapitated bodies, the burning luggage, and even the bodies of young children. Within five minutes, though, the Tactical Patrol Force—elite cops who responded to major events like riots, parades, and (sadly) plane crashes—was on scene, led by one of the legendary chiefs in the history of the NYPD, Ray McDermott, a true cop's cop. He gave the order, "Kick ass and take names. No arrests." He would not tolerate looting of the dead. He had big balls even though he had once been demoted by Commissioner Patrick Murphy, only to return to his deserved glory. In short order, TPF secured the scene, sending the cowardly looters scrambling like the vermin they were.

With a large area around the crashed jetliner secured from public view, we began our job of inspecting each apparent victim to determine whether he or she could or could not be helped, and none in this crash even made it alive to an ambulance, so we began the grim task of tagging and bagging.

Each piece of a body had to be individually tagged with a 9-5 tag, the official NYPD tag that is affixed to the big toe of those who die on the mean streets of the Big Apple. I know you have seen them at one time or another on A&E or some cop show when they have pulled a body out of the freezer in the morgue. After they open the door, it is the first thing you see as they pull the clean, crisp, white sheet back, exposing the victim's toe. It has all the biographical information of the victim on it, including time of death, name, address, and what the medical examiner felt was the cause of death.

Thinking back, I can still smell the stench in the Bellevue morgue. It was like the sweet smell of a melon gone bad. This was just one of many smells of the corpses I encountered. The smells depend on the stage of decomposition. The first ones are an unreal smell. But I did have numerous DOAs in the later stages of decomposition. They smelled like leather, or a mummy.

It was a long and tiring night. Wreckage, luggage, bodies, and body parts were strewn everywhere. It was our job to put all the pieces back together.

By midmorning the next day, the bodies were at the Queens medical examiner's office—the morgue. We were relieved by ESU units from the Queens ESU squads—Truck 10 and Truck 9. They would continue the grid search for remains and body parts just in case we missed anything. Gary and I were heading back to the Fiftieth Precinct, where our ESU

Truck 4 squad was quartered. I decided not to go home. I would be due back for a four-by-twelve shift soon. It was already 1:00 p.m., so there was no sense driving back to Brooklyn, which was some thirty-two miles away. I took a shower and then went to the corner bar. Every precinct had one. This one was called Pauline's, and it had great burgers and the coldest draft beer in the Bronx. I felt I deserved a break and some downtime. I ate two great cheeseburgers and had a couple of drafts. The news on television was reporting that the crash of Eastern Airlines flight 66 from New Orleans was apparently caused by wind shear. All 112 aboard were killed.

I returned to quarters and sat around the gray table with the guys for a while and then took a nap. As I lay back, I thought about how difficult it must have been for the families of the victims. But I was glad on one point—they didn't have to see them as I did. I hoped for a closed coffin. As I fell into a restless sleep, I wondered what lay ahead for me at 4:00 p.m., the start of my next four-by-twelve in Truck 4. It would be just another day in the ESU.

Chapter Eight

THE FIRST TIME

...Jumper on the Brooklyn Bridge

I was always very proud to work in New York City. It is the most special city on earth. People do not realize how special it is. Its wonderfully diverse population of people from all over the world and its different neighborhoods make you feel that you are visiting other countries. And its boundless offerings of culture, sports, entertainment, parks, rivers, and majestic architecture that are found nowhere else in the world are truly inspiring. The Big Apple is a beautiful city.

It is a city surrounded by water: the Atlantic Ocean, the majestic Hudson River, the East River, Harlem River, Long Island Sound, New York Bay, Jamaica Bay, thousands of creeks, and even lakes in the manmade Central and Prospect parks. Being surrounded by bodies of water meant that the city's lifeblood—its residents and commuters and its truckloads of food, oil, and equipment—needed bridges to make the city work.

And it has some beauties: the classic George Washington, which connects Manhattan to New Jersey; the Verrazano Narrows Bridge, which connects Brooklyn to Staten Island (you have to take another bridge to get off that island and into New Jersey); and the Triborough

Bridge, which connects Manhattan to the Bronx and Queens (Queens and Brooklyn are on the island of Long Island). Only the Bronx is connected to the mainland U.S. There are also the Whitestone and Throgs Neck bridges, which connect the Bronx to Queens and a bunch of highway bridges spanning some of the waterways within the city.

The most famous of all these bridges, of course, is the Brooklyn Bridge, which connects Manhattan to Brooklyn. It, more than any other bridge, is responsible for turning New York City into a major metropolitan complex, and it stands as a symbol for Gotham at its most progressive. It is one of five bridges that link Manhattan's East Side with Brooklyn and Queens. The others are the Williamsburg Bridge, the Manhattan Bridge, the Queensborough Bridge (also known as the Fifty-ninth Street Bridge), and the aforementioned Triborough Bridge. But none has the romance, the beauty, and the place in American history of the Brooklyn Bridge, which was opened in 1883 and, from its first hour, has been an iconic image of the Big Apple.

Every E-Man gets to know the Brooklyn Bridge intimately. Maybe it is due to all that romance, lore, and magnetism, but the Brooklyn Bridge is a favorite place for unfortunate people bent on hurting themselves. "Jumper on the Brooklyn Bridge" is a common radio call heard by E-Men.

The New York Police Department receives hundreds of calls each year for people attempting suicide by jumping off bridges, buildings, and other high structures. The Brooklyn Bridge leads the league in attracting those who want to do themselves in, with probably about 150 a year. These days it is considered a prime target for a terrorist attack because of its iconic symbolism, and NYPD surveillance cameras are stationed on the bridge 24/7.

Aside from its fame, it is an easy bridge to get onto. It has a very accessible pedestrian walkway, and its old-fashioned steelwork affords many substantial footholds for those foolhardy or desperate enough to want to make the climb toward the edge over the East River.

I climbed the cables and railings of the Brooklyn Bridge more than fifty times in my career. Each time I marveled at the view from up there: the lower Manhattan skyscrapers to the west, New York Bay, the

Atlantic Ocean to the south, and Long Island to the east. We used to practice jumper prevention on the Verazzano, which is higher and longer and gives more of a feeling of being out in the wild country than does the Brooklyn, but most of our action came on the old bridge whose roadway runs right past city hall.

The first time I went up was in the fall of 1974. It was an Indian summer day, warm with a bright sun in a cloudless sky. I was "flying" that day; that is, as a virtual rookie, I was assigned to fill a spot for an E-Man who was out sick or on vacation. I did that a lot in my first year; so much, in fact, that I bought a ball cap with silver wings attached to the sides, kind of like Mercury. I sewed an ESU patch on the front. I called it my Flying Hat. Most of the guys got a kick out of it, although some old-timers didn't appreciate my sense of humor.

I arrived at the truck early, as was my habit throughout my career. I loved the job so much I never minded coming in early or staying late.

My regular assignment was with Truck 4 in the Bronx, but that day I was flying to Truck 1, or the Hollywood Truck, as it's known in Manhattan. I was like a kid in a candy store. All the great jobs that Truck 1 had been involved in made it a legend. I couldn't wait to get there, even though it was for only one day. Several years later, I would be assigned to Truck 1 on a regular basis.

As I pulled into the East Twenty-first Street headquarters, I saw Richie Powers standing out front. He was known as Mr. Emergency. Richie was one of my heroes, along with Jack Casey and Jack Shea. Richie earned that nickname for his great rescues in Truck 1. I felt like a kid called up from the minor leagues; it was like I would be playing the outfield alongside Mickey Mantle, my other hero while growing up in Manhattan. Richie extended his hand. "Hey kid, welcome aboard, you're working with me today."

I said, "Great! It's an honor to be working with you, Rich."

He told me that he had already checked out the truck, so we rolled. We were assigned to Boy 1, the smaller truck. Our area of patrol was Manhattan South, which covered perhaps the most famous and glamorous territory in the world: Times Square, Fifth Avenue, Rockefeller Center, The Empire State Building, Broadway, Madison

Square Garden, Grand Central Terminal, Penn Station, Studio 54, the Copacabana, the headquarters of all the major television networks, the *New York Times*, the *Daily News*, city hall, The Waldorf Astoria, The Plaza—this list could go on forever and still leave a lot of famous places out. It was truly a patrol zone that never slept; a place where celebrities mixed with Bowery bums, gangsters with cops, and priests with strippers, and where the average New Yorker worked, played, and sometimes got into serious trouble.

The adrenalin rush experienced while barreling full steam, sirens wailing, air horns blaring, and emergency lights flashing like crazy is impossible to describe. I have jumped out of airplanes in enemy-infested jungles. I have survived combat, both in war and on the streets of New York. But to me, sitting in an emergency service truck with the eyes of the world on you in Manhattan South beats anything a person can experience, even a thrill seeker such as myself.

The tour that evening began slowly. Richie was a great teacher, and as he drove, he kept up a steady monologue of information about the division. He explained how best to move around the congested streets in the theater district, where to park the rig at different precincts we might have to visit, certain buildings where security sucked, and others where the doormen were helpful. He knew where some celebrities lived and where certain politicians drank. He knew where actors got into trouble and where commuting businessmen might stop for a drink on the way home. Those are the kinds of things cops know. It is the information they ingest and call up when rushing to a radio run or watching a suspicious guy walk down a certain street.

Our first job that night was a 10-30—a robbery in progress. The address was Mama Leone's, a popular Italian restaurant in the theater district. The dispatcher added, "Possible perp trapped." Richie negotiated the traffic like the pro he was. Leone's was a tourist trap; very popular every night of the week. If a hard-assed perp got himself jammed up in there, it could mean anything from a shootout with innocent victims in the line of fire to a hostage job.

As we pulled up, the street was jammed with onlookers gawking at the number of precinct units that had already arrived on the scene and the loud presence our arrival caused. Richie pulled to the curb across the street from the restaurant and ordered me to suit up. In the ESU, that meant heavy vests and heavy weapons. I chose my favorite, the cut-down Ithaca DeerSlayer 12-gauge shotgun. As usual, I loaded a slug first and double-aught buck next. Was I going to shoot someone this night? Possibly. The thought did not go through my mind. I just prepared myself for any eventuality, and a gunfight was one of the possible scenarios. That's not macho bullshit; that is reality.

When a patrol cop gets shot, it is usually a biff-bam-bang situation—fast; all thinking was instinctive. He rolls up to a scene and shots are fired. For E-Men, it is a little different. We had some idea of what we were walking into. But training takes the hesitation out of you. You drill so often and think so much about possible deadly encounters that you enter the fray more like a big game hunter than a fast-moving cop.

Richie and I approached the main entrance. As we entered, I could hear the War Wagon, Truck 2, approach and pull to the curb. Its crew joined us as we went into the restaurant. The precinct cops had done a good job of emptying the place out. They briefed us that they believed the perp had fled, with a few dollars from the cash register, through a side door into an alley.

That may or may not have been accurate information. It was what they truly believed, but Richie Powers knew we would have to make that determination, so we continued in. I was in front, Richie alongside and a step to the rear of me, and the Truck 2 guys behind him. The restaurant was normally a dark place that used candles on the tables, and no one had turned on the lights.

We made our way through the dining room and into the kitchen, which by the way was the filthiest kitchen I had ever seen in my life. After about ten minutes of looking into every closet, under every table, and behind every pot, we were satisfied that the perp had made his getaway. This was a job for the detectives. We slowly came down from our state of high anxiety. We called these times "shits and giggles moments." Back in the street, we took off our vests and put up our weapons. No one would die in Mama Leone's this night, at least not from gunshot wounds.

We kibitzed with the precinct cops, astonished to find out that they sometimes actually ate food from that filthy kitchen, as we filled out the forms required to document the job, as was demanded by ESU regulations.

Every assignment was documented. The record books read like a scorecard at a Ripley's Believe It or Not! museum: auto extraction, barricaded perp, jumper, person under a train, finger cut off in a machine, infant's head stuck in a toilet bowl, teenager impaled on a fence, domestic dispute ending in murder-suicide, newlyweds trapped in an elevator. That says it all. That is the world of the ESU. All we had to do was survive the job, check the boxes, and fill out the forms.

Richie and I were no sooner buckled up back in the truck than the citywide frequency screamed out at us. "Truck 1, Adam 1, Boy 1 . . . confirmed jumper, Brooklyn Bridge, precinct units on the scene."

My heart skipped a beat and then started racing a mile a minute. My first jumper on the Brooklyn Bridge! This had suddenly become a night to remember. I and the great Richie Powers were headed downtown to the goddamn Brooklyn Bridge to save some poor soul from destroying his or her life and messing up the East River.

Richie threw on all the lights and sirens and put his pedal to the metal. We roared across Forty-second Street, the street of dreams. I knew thousands of people were looking at us as we headed east. I loved being the center of their attention as I went about God's work. Someone was in trouble, and Al and Richie were the cavalry coming to the rescue across Forty-second Street.

Richie knew this territory like he knew his own bedroom. We scattered the traffic at Times Square—the crossroads of the world—and in less than two minutes were on the FDR Drive, heading south. I was not conscious of it, but of course Richie knew there was an exit from the drive that would take us right onto the Brooklyn-bound side of the bridge. Truck 1 and Adam 1 were not far behind us. We were a rescue convoy. At the same time, the precinct guys and highway patrol guys were clearing the bridge and closing it down from both sides. They all waited for us to appear and save the day. Well, actually, not everyone was anxious for us to get there. Truck 8 from Brooklyn also claimed the bridge as its territory, and the dispatcher would have caught hell if he had not called those units to the scene. We heard the call. "Truck 8, Boy 8; respond to the jumper job on the Brooklyn Bridge." Then we heard them answer. "Truck 8, responding." "Boy 8, ETA under a minute."

Of course, we knew they would be heading there as soon as they heard us call. We would be on scene in a minute or two. This was an ongoing friendly feud between the Manhattan units and our Brooklyn counterparts. Remember that the bridge connects Manhattan and Brooklyn, so competition was always inevitable. I, being a flyboy this evening, had no particular long-range stake in the feud, but I wanted this job. It was my first. I was with Powers, and I was born to do this.

The precinct guys were informing division radio that the jumper was climbing the Manhattan tower, which was our goddamn territory—if we got there first, that is. As we approached the ramp that would take us onto the bridge, I grabbed the binoculars and quickly spotted the jumper near the top of perhaps the most recognizable bridge tower in the world. To me he looked like a fly climbing chicken wire.

As we pulled up to the base of the Manhattan tower, I could see Truck 8 approaching from the Brooklyn side. We beat them. They would now take a backup position and join us on the high cables if needed. Or they could set up an airbag and coordinate with the harbor units that were arriving in the waters below.

Richie said, "Al, get your Morrisey belt and a length of lifeline, and don't forget your gloves. I'll go up first . . . you follow close, and keep yourself hooked onto the cables!" Powers had been here before, and I had a feeling of well-being and pride come over me, as I sensed that he trusted me to do my job and would look out for me if he could.

I was not afraid at all about what we were about to do. I was never afraid of heights. I enjoyed climbing rocks and parachute towers at Ft. Campbell. I had practiced on the Verazzano Bridge, from which you could see as far as the horizon. It was a thrill to me. The challenge gave me a rush! I went right at it. As we climbed, I stayed close behind Richie. I knew he had done this dozens of times. I didn't want him worrying about me. We had a person bent on suicide waiting for us. There would come a day that an ESU rookie would be following me up the cables, but that was down the road.

As we climbed toward the Manhattan tower, I looked below. A tugboat was passing under the bridge. *Shit,* I thought, *that looks so small.* Every footstep was taken with caution. Actually, to climb, you need to walk like a duck, pointing your feet outward; it's step, grab the cable, and reattach your lifeline . . . slowly. One errant move and you would do a "Brodie."

Anyone who grew up in NYC knows what a Brodie is; he was a fellow from the 1880s who jumped from the Brooklyn Bridge and lived. But he was a lucky one. Hitting the water is like hitting concrete.

As we climbed the tower, I noticed that the cables were getting much higher above my head, making it impossible to hook onto them. So this meant that the last twenty feet of the climb was a free climb. There was no place to hook onto for security. The Brooklyn Bridge is constructed with a ladder just below the top of the tower. You climb into the tower and climb the ladder that leads to the top of the tower. So there we were, on top of the Manhattan tower. We had a young man above us who wanted to end it all. And I was not convinced that he didn't want to take a couple of cops along for the dive.

This guy was standing on the edge of the tower, complaining about whatever was wrong in his life. He was woeful—talking fast, but more mumbling than making himself clear. Suddenly, as Richie got within a few feet of the man, he broke out into this unbelievable Irish brogue. I thought I'd piss my pants. Richie sounded like Spencer Tracy in *Boys Town.* I wondered how many times he had used this approach. This was the definition of on-the-job training.

Between the wind, my heart pumping, and the other harbor noises, I actually could not hear what Richie was saying, but in a couple of minutes he had the guy, who was Hispanic, ready to take communion.

Within ten minutes, our jumper agreed to go down. But in the ESU, a jumper must be secured. So out came the cuffs. Our man had a shitfit, and I thought we would have to wrestle the cuffs onto him.

We were hundreds of feet in the air, not hooked onto the cable, and now he was giving us trouble. But Father Powers prevailed and calmed him down. And with the Truck 8 crew, who by now had joined us as backup, we were able to cuff him in a matter of seconds. It was a little hairy rolling around with him. There isn't much room to play on the top of the Brooklyn Bridge tower. Before my career was over, I would climb the Brooklyn Bridge more than fifty times on successful rescue missions.

Well, my tour with Father Powers was a plus in my ESU career. As I was going back to the Bronx, he asked me if I had a lightweight ESU jacket. All I had was the winter jacket. He said, "Kid . . . come back into quarters." Richie opened his locker and gave me his summer jacket. I still have it to this day, thirty years later. I still keep in contact with Richie. He has recently moved from Florida to North Carolina, where he lives in the same neighborhood as his daughter. He was truly Mr. Emergency. It was my honor to have ridden a tour with a guy known as Mr. Emergency.

There are other ESU cops who hold a special place in my heart and mind. I can still, after all these years, hear their gentle reprimands, their artful way of teaching a new guy the ropes, their self-effacing humor. I worked with guys like Jack Casey, Bobby Benz, Eddie Yano, Ronnie "Ra Ra" King, and, of course, the legendary Jack Shea.

These were the first E-Men I met and the first that treated me as a part of the ESU team. This is not to say the other old-timers were not okay. But when I was the new kid and these guys were WWII veterans, mostly Irish guys from Northern Manhattan and the Bronx, they were the kind of men I held in high esteem.

They always reminded me of my uncle Jack Flynn, a West Side guy who won the Navy Cross while serving with the marines on Iwo Jima and received a Silver Star before the war was over. If they only knew my uncle Jack, he would have been accepted into the E-Man fraternity.

I remembered him coming home on leave from WWII when I was a kid. He wore marine winter greens and a garrison belt. He was a tough-as-nails guy with a heart of gold, like most of my comrades in the ESU. These kinds of men were my heroes, and to grow up and actually get to race through the city streets with them, to climb bridges with them, and to face down gunmen with them at my side was a dream come true. I was a very lucky man.

Of all the times I went up the Brooklyn Bridge, only once was for a reason other than a jumper. One day a tourist enjoying the spectacular view from the bridge's pedestrian walkway, which ran right down the center of the magnificent structure, was killed when a cable snapped and swung wildly through the crowd. He was almost cut in two. The walkway was constructed mostly of wood, and the cable snapped with such force it ripped right through it.

My partner and I were ordered to secure the loose cable. This was a very dangerous assignment. The cable was made of copper; it was six inches thick, and about eighty feet of it was swinging wildly in the wind. It was a Sunday around noon, and it was a miracle that no one else was hurt. There wasn't anything we could do to save the poor tourist, so we got right to the task of capturing the loose cable. We had to fight a strong wind as we climbed about forty feet to where the cable was close enough to grab.

It took about thirty minutes, and we were lucky not to get dumped into the drink or knocked down to the walkway as we got the job done and turned over the now tied-down cable to the city workers, who actually knew what to do with it.

With that job, we made the front page of the *Daily News*—not an unusual place for an E-Man's picture to be.

Barricaded suspect who fired at police taken into custody

Chief of Department Robert J. Johnston Jr. awarding
Al Sheppard "Cop of the Month"

Bombs placed at Penn Station Manhattan, Al Sheppard removing device

Assisting the Bomb Squad

Bomb Removal Robot, c. 1985

Paul Redeca and Al Sheppard securing
broken cable on the Brooklyn Bridge

My older son, Al, Cardinal Cooke and me at Saint Patrick's Cathedral

Mother's Day fire rescue, 1985, Brooklyn, New York

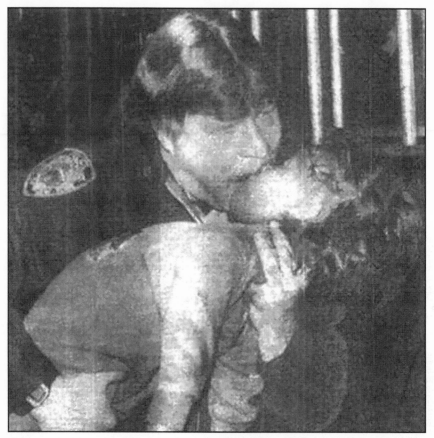

Mother's Day fire rescue, 1985, Brooklyn, New York

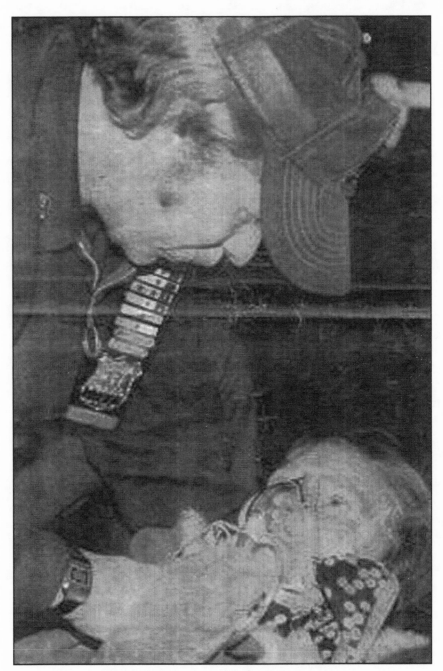

Administering oxygen to an elderly woman

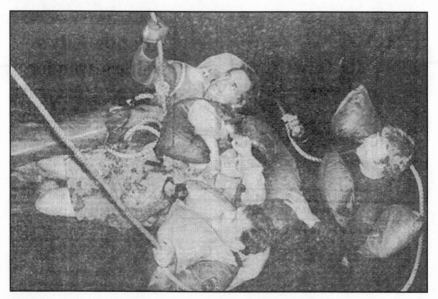

Water rescue, East River, New York

Gary Gorman and Al Sheppard, members of
NYPD Anti-terrorist Team c. 1977

First NYPD rappel from a helicopter at ESU
Specialized Training School c. 1977

Bringing down a jumper safely

First NYDP ESU truck

Paul Ragonese and Al Sheppard receiving oxygen after fire rescue

NYPD Anti-terrorist Team
Bobby Benz, Frank Gallagher, Lt. Larry Savage, Lt. Swanson, Jack Casey, Sgt.
Botkin, Capt. Ray Hanratty XO of ESU, Al Sheppard, Gary Gorman
(others unknown)

Truck 1 Manhattan

Prince Street

Detectives James Tedaldi and Al Sheppard (l-r) Consultants (NYPD, Retired)

Al's partner in the Intelligence Division, Det. First Grade James Tedaldi, and Al Sheppard with the NBC/Warner Brothers TV show Prince Street

Searching for gunmen with Bill Fox

Confronting a sniper in Brooklyn with Bill Pisask and Tommy Barns, Truck 8

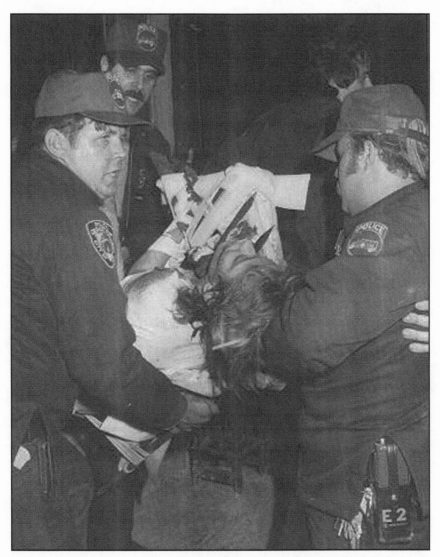

*Girl impaled on fence, James Gaffney (dec.), Sgt. Bill Friedlander,
and Al Sheppard, Truck 2*

Crew of Truck 1, c. 1985, with the legendary Mike McCorroy (arms crossed)

Paul Redeca and Al Sheppard removing jumper from Williamsburg Bridge

The ESU Armored Rescue Vehicle c. 1985
(previously known as the "Rescue Ambulance")

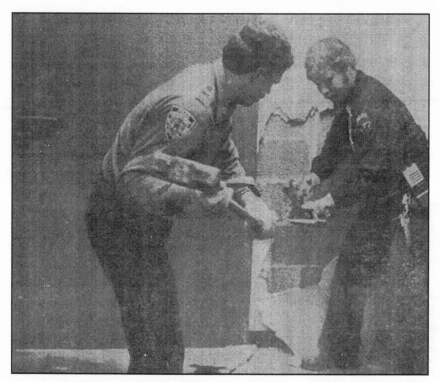

*Paul Ragonese and Al Sheppard breaking into a safe to rescue
a child locked in by accident*

Chapter Nine

THE JUMPERS

... *It was a freezing night*

The George Washington Bridge is one of the most beautiful in the world. I climbed it many times and always looked in wonder at what appeared to be the toy cars on the highways down below and the breathtaking view of the majestic Hudson River as it passes under the bridge on its way to the Atlantic Ocean. In the other direction, it flows from beautiful Upstate New York, and thankfully it is now being restored to its rightful natural glory.

A jumper on the George Washington ties up traffic for miles around, as it is a major highway link into the city. When it occurs during rush hours, commuters sit and stew in the cars as we go about our business of saving lives. I know that many of them just wish the guy will jump so they can get started on their way to work. I understand that.

One chilly fall morning, Gary Gorman and I got the call to respond to the George Washington. It was still dark when we got there, but already the drive-time radio traffic reporters were warning commuters to find an alternate route into the city. We reached the jumper pretty easily. He had parked his car and then started to climb. This was the first time I had one park and climb. Usually when you find a car on the bridge, you find a suicide note on the seat and the driver in the water. But he found that climbing up was not as easy as we make it look, and he did not get up very high before we arrived directly below him.

He did not want to fight us or argue. He just wanted to end it all. "Why don't you guys leave me alone," he said. We are trained to treat these kinds of incidents almost as hostage negotiations; one ESU officer tries to make conversation with the person. If the jumper doesn't relate to that particular officer, another one tries to make a relationship. I have never lost a jumper, and I was able to get this depressed man in his business suit and tie to talk with me.

The first thing he told me was that he was a famous businessman. He owned a big store in Manhattan that was a household name. But he said his family life sucked. He couldn't get along with his wife and kids. I always felt that the majority of jumpers were calling out for help, saying, "Look at me; I need somebody to hear my pain."

Usually we have more fake jumpers than actual ones. If they decided to end their lives, they wouldn't wait for the ESU to respond. In addition, it seemed that we had the majority of jumpers around the Christmas season and just after; mostly single people with no family or friends. I often wondered how bad it could be. I learned when I was fighting cancer in 2002 how bad it can get.

If it wasn't for my wife, Patricia; my children; and my good friends' support, I don't think I could have fought the fight. And much of what I learned about human nature as I tried to save people's lives as they stood on bridges or rooftops or at their windows, bent on killing themselves, came in handy as I fought my personal survival battle.

I was able to talk almost everyone down. If I knew that the dialogue wasn't going to work, there was only one way to get the job done. I had to make a grab. I would never hesitate to go for "The Grab." I made sure I had enough of a lifeline to extend beyond the jumper and that I was tied to something securely. On a command or signal, I would go for the grab.

If you went over the side with the jumper, you had your brother E-Men there. Most came without a struggle. For some it was a life-and-death confrontation. There were a few times that I thought the jumper might take us all over the side. You must remember that there are two types of jumpers. Both are mentally unstable. One is depressed over some life situation, divorce, money, etc. Then you have the out-and-out psycho. In my opinion, it was always easier to confront the depressed person, like the businessman on the George Washington that chilly morning. The out-and-out psycho is irrational. He doesn't care if he takes you with him. Also, these types seem to be and act as if they are superhuman. I think it is a chemical reaction.

An eighty-five-pound woman once flipped me like I was a rag doll. We had gone in for the the grab. She had her infant at the window, and she was going to take them both to the street below. My sergeant gave me the nod; he grabbed for the infant, and I tried to put her in a bear hug. The next thing I knew, I was on the floor. Thankfully we were able to save both the baby and her.

But on the George Washington that day, I was able to hit the right chord with the businessman. I talked to him about how much he had to live for and how many people he would sadden with his death—not only his family, but his friends and employees and the customers who loved his famous store as well. Finally, the cold and my harping and, of course, his better judgment won out, and he agreed to come down. "How do we do this?" he asked, as if realizing for the first time that he was hundreds of feet above the mighty Hudson River. Gary came up on my signal, and we put him between us and then slowly, step by step, took him down. An ambulance was waiting on the roadway to take him to the psycho ward. But he was not a psycho, and he spent that night in his own bed with his loving family after being examined at the hospital. Everyone finally got to work okay and probably bragged to their friends that they saw us save the man's life.

About as different in atmosphere from the sleek George Washington Bridge in upper Manhattan is the Williamsburg Bridge, which connects Delancey Street on the Lower East Side to Brooklyn; one crowded, gritty urban area to another.

In December of 1984, on a "cold as a witch's tit" night, I met a Vietnam vet named Sammy on the top of the Manhattan Tower of the Williamsburg Bridge.

Sammy was a Hispanic man, and the first thing he told me as I approached him in the freezing darkness was that he was a post traumatic stress patient. He was suffering from the trauma of Vietnam. This was a guy I was not going to lose.

My partner that night was Paul Redeca. Paul was a huge man—at least 6' 5" and two hundred plus pounds. We often kidded him that his head was as big as a basketball. And that was the truth. Paul was a dedicated ESU officer, but he looked like a huge Cabbage Patch Kid. He was the brunt of many jokes, and he took them well. Paul was truly a gentle giant.

Paul carried every tool possible. This is where a lot of his ribbing came from. We called his gun belt, which was loaded with scissors and anything else you could imagine, the "Charlie Car," referring to one of the ESU units that would carry backup equipment.

That night, as we climbed the Williamsburg Bridge, the wind was stinging our faces. The climb wasn't difficult, aside from the effects of the weather conditions and the occasional patch of ice. There, sitting like an Indian around a campfire, was Sammy, right smack dab in the center of the steel tower. I thought he was praying. He didn't even know Paul and I were there. Paul, not one for wasting time, pounced with his huge frame on Sammy and had him cuffed in a matter of seconds. We relaxed for a few minutes before making the climb back down.

I was able to talk to this guy. He was well dressed and highly intelligent. He had been having problems with the VA over his medication. I told him I had a friend there and would make a call to the VA Hospital on East Twenty-first Street on his behalf. That was the first thing I did in the morning. I know what it is to fight your own demons. But this story doesn't have a happy ending. About a week later, Sammy was back on top of the WBB. I wasn't working that day. I was told he asked if Paul or I were working before he jumped. Sammy's demons had won; he became another victim of Vietnam.

There were so many occasions on which my partners and I climbed high up over the streets or rivers to rescue people in distress that after all these years, they run together in my mind. I don't know why I remember some like they occurred yesterday and others just vaguely. Rescuing a jumper never becomes routine, but it does become so much of the job of the E-Man that after a while it blends in with the drivers trapped in overturned cars and the possible hostage situations that never amount to much.

One night that I especially remember was in January 1979. I was assigned to Truck 2 in Harlem. We covered Manhattan from Fifty-ninth Street, river-to-river and north to the Bronx line. My partner (once again Gary Gorman) and I were working a midnight shift. That meant we started our tour at midnight and ended at 8:00 a.m. It was a freezing night—raw and wet with high winds. Our first job was a person trapped in an automobile on the West Side Highway at 135th Street. It was so cold we almost couldn't start the engine for the Hurst tool—the lifesaving piece of equipment the media dubbed the Jaws of Life because of the way it separates victims from what is about to kill them by spreading its jaws like an alligator. I always carried a can of Quick Start, the spray that assists in starting troublesome engines. One shot into the breather and *boom!* the Jaws were ready to operate.

In all of our jobs, every minute counts, but this is especially true when we are charged with extracting a victim from an automobile. Usually, we cannot get close enough to the poor soul to get a certain assessment of his or her injuries. They could be pouring blood where we can't see, and the EMS guys cannot even reach a place to take a pulse. Often, they are unconscious. Their lives depended on ESU officers performing a safe and timely removal so advanced medical attention could be administered. That night we got the guy out in time, and Gary and I returned to Truck 2's quarters on West 126th Street, just off Broadway.

This was not the Broadway of bright lights and Forty-second Street where the Hollywood Truck, Truck 1, was usually found. We were so far away we might as well have been in a different city. The Broadway of Harlem, with dead rats rotting in the gutters and glass from broken beer bottles covering the landscape, was mostly lined with broken-down apartment buildings in which most of the inhabitants were hard-working, law-abiding citizens, but many of their neighbors were strung-out drug addicts and dirt-poor people who had been beaten up by life and would take it out on anyone around them.

To a cop, it was an area of drug-obsessed blight where child abuse calls were mixed with domestic violence and irrational shootings.

The first thing I did when I got to quarters was to run hot water over my numb hands. On a night like this, gloves didn't even help. I got a hot cup of coffee while Gary changed his pants, which he discovered were disintegrating from battery acid spilled at the scene of the trapped driver.

As we sat down at the gray table, I said "Hey Gary, you're lucky it didn't eat through to your balls."

Jimmy Gaffney, already sitting with a cup of coffee, jokingly shouted across the table, "Hey Al, that would be the case if he had any."

It doesn't sound very funny now, but that kind of baseless humor was what often brought us down from the adrenalin highs of working a rescue.

In every ESU quarters, there is a gray table. It sits in the center of the kitchen. This is where everything was discussed; the table was used for critiquing jobs, personal gripes, and just shooting the shit. As I look back over the years, I see that it was during these discussions that I was changing from the young kid who wanted to help everyone to a hardened, professional E-Man who, while gaining expertise in saving lives and stopping bad guys in their tracks, might have been losing a little of his own humanity.

Those bullshit sessions, with the joking, the putting down of each other, and the criticizing of the bosses at 1 PP (Police Plaza) were too often defense mechanisms used to cover our real feelings and mask the concerns of our own collective conscience.

Gary was about to pour another cup of coffee when the squawk box intruded. "Adam 2, respond to the area of West 125th Street and Twelfth Avenue; report of a jumper."

Coffee mug down, cigarette extinguished, sweaters and gloves pulled on, Gorman and I took the stairs that led to the truck bays three at a time. We would be there in less than a minute.

Now the weather was really getting bad. Sleet and freezing rain were blowing horizontally. This particular location was always busy with meat delivery trucks unloading from all over the country. Its official name was Manhattan Valley—a reminder of when the city was growing northward. It is actually a valley, and it is the home of one of the two fault lines that run through the island of Manhattan. To bridge the gap in Manhattan Valley, a large, elevated viaduct was constructed to enable Riverside Drive to continue to the northern part of Manhattan.

The structure appeared ancient the day it was built; it was painted battleship gray, and it had several overhangs and decorated steel girders. This night it was coated with ice, which reflected the brilliance of our flashing emergency lights. On arrival, we searched the immediate area with flood lights. We couldn't find anything. Then a trucker with a thick Tennessee brogue appeared out of the now-blinding sleet.

He said, "Officer, I heard someone calling for help up there!"

Following his lead, we headed down the street toward the on ramp for the southbound West Side Highway, which runs parallel to Riverside Drive, along the Hudson River. The closer we got to the river, the worse the weather seemed to get, but from that side, looking up, we could see a small figure huddled in the superstructure of the viaduct approximately eighty feet above the cobblestone street. "How did she get up there?" the trucker shouted above the noise of the wind.

I told him I had no idea and then said, "My problem is how the hell we're going to get her down."

In the back of my mind I concurred with the trucker. This would be a murderous climb. It wasn't just the weather; it was the configuration of the structure.

Here is where the training in the ESU was invaluable. We were always taught to think on our feet. There is no one way to get a job done. I called central. "Have Truck 8 respond with the air bag truck." This was a large van that carried a large inflatable air bag. It also carried a generator and two large fans that kept the air bag inflated.

As part of our training, we were required to jump onto the air bag several times. Many a life was saved by this piece of equipment.

I made the decision to relocate to the top of the viaduct. It would be safer to go over the side and go down to make the rescue than it would be to try to climb up the slippery metal framework. We took the truck a few blocks around to get up to the top.

107

As Gary and I reached the top, the wind and sleet became even more intense; it was stinging our faces at every turn. We tried to make contact with the person, but the hellish weather conditions made it impossible.

By stretching my body while holding on with one hand and shielding my face with the other, I could see over the side. I couldn't believe what I saw. The jumper was an elderly woman. She was clutching the superstructure, clearly not wanting to fall or jump. I wondered how long she could hold on. We had to act instantly.

"You or me?" asked Gary, but before I could finish my sentence, he had his Morrissey belt on. We quickly laid out a plan to lower Gary to the woman. She was maybe fifteen feet from the top. Clearly she had climbed over the top, not up from the street as the trucker first thought. I tied the lifeline to the heavy-duty bumper of our truck. I gave Gary twenty feet of line to play with. I was sure that would be enough. Over the side he went. Using our portable radios, he advised me as to how far to lower him.

A new problem arose. From where we were making our descent, the woman was unreachable. There was a distance of some six feet between her and Gary. But though he was not exactly on his feet, Gary still was capable of making a quick decision. He would make an attempt to swing over to her position. That decision later became a joke between Gary and me. I never let him live down his report over the radio: "I'm swinging now." More jerky cop humor to hide the fact that we were both scared shitless for his life, as well as the jumper's.

Gary made it on the first attempt—a great job. Now I had to deal with getting both of them to the top safely. In order to be hoisted up, they would have to swing freely until they were at street level. I radioed to Gary, "Is she secure?"

"10-4 . . . let's go up," was his welcome answer.

I placed the truck in reverse. Slowly—ever so slowly—I inched her back. Up until this time, Gary and I were alone on the viaduct; the weather was slowing everyone's response. From the cab of the truck, I could not see what progress they were making as I backed up. But then I was joined by another E-Man. He raced to the safety railing. Now I was directed by his hand signals. Within a minute or two, both Gary and the jumper were back on solid ground. We packed her off to St. Luke's Hospital, where she was treated for hypothermia.

We never knew how she got herself into that predicament or why. She was unable to speak English. As in most cases, we never got to follow up on the lives of the people we rescued. We never learned what made them so desperate. After a time, they became numbers in our record book—statistics for the chiefs to make some sense of while we waited for the dispatcher to order us to our next nightmare.

Chapter Ten

THE MURDER OF CECIL SLEDGE

. . . Report of a police officer shot

The winter of 1980 was typical for New York City, with just enough snow to keep the streets looking dirty and to make it difficult to park, and with that biting cold that turns the wind into a weapon as you try to go about your life while waiting for spring to arrive.

It is said that bad weather is a cop's best friend, and I would not argue much with that. It is true that street crime goes down in the winter; there are just fewer targets for the street thugs to pick on. Even the homeless, when the temperature goes below freezing, find warm spots in shelters to wait out the warming sun, which in New York comes along just around baseball season, in early April.

For a cop walking a beat, the freeze is brutal. In the days just before lightweight down coats arrived on the scene, some guys still wore those long, woolen overcoats that worked fine for about one hundred years in the NYPD. Sometimes the guy on the beat would pull his scarf around his mouth, and some cops wore ear muffs, which I always thought looked nerdy. Like a jerk, I would suffer with frozen, red ears.

Of course, we all looked for inside spots, such as a candy store or a coffee shop, where we could quickly warm up and still make the checkpoints, where the sergeant and his driver would roll up in their warm RMP with the book we had to sign. Some would bring some coffee. Some, if you were close enough and trusting enough, would offer something a little more warming, but in all those years, I never would partake of it.

I was in the ESU by this time, assigned in the Bronx with the great Gary Gorman as a partner. We were working the four-by-twelve. For the ESU, the winter brought more car accidents and more serious falls, but fewer jumpers and crowd control situations. We were able to stay warm in the headquarters garage or in our heated trucks, and while on the outside, our usual output of energy kept us warm. Sometimes, when we were in the real cold during a call that was heavy on manual labor, such as getting someone out of an overturned car, we would sweat so much under our clothes that we risked frostbite if we did not get back and change into drier uniforms.

On this particular January morning, I started out the day very early, working at my moonlight job. Like most cops, I was always broke. We just did not make enough money to provide for our families. That's an issue that today's cops continue to struggle with. Most of us married young and had more than one kid and were not crazy about having our wives work.

Of course, we did not think about that when we joined up. Most just thought about the safety of a civil service job—its great health benefits and retirement at an early age. You would be surprised how many cops had also taken the civil service test to be firefighters and sanitation workers. They were cops because NYPD called first. I knew friends who transferred to the fire department after a few years, and vice versa. These cops did not do their jobs with any less dedication or vigor than those, such as me, who joined for the adventure and the desire to serve the public.

Once anyone put that blue uniform on, the people of the city of New York could be sure they would get the service they deserved. Of course, there were exceptions: some cops who were little better than the mutts they arrested, and some that were worse. They also made the front pages of the newspapers and got the jail time they deserved.

But, my good friends Cecil "Frank" Sledge and Mike Duffy were the real McCoys. They were smart, professional lawmen who gave their all to the city and their fellow men in blue. Unfortunately, dedication and valor does not pay the mortgage.

So Frank, Mike, and I earned some extra bucks by doing house renovations. We were all strong and had some skills in carpentry, plumbing, and electrical work. It was just enough to make some extra cash as handymen.

We were a hardy bunch of tough, strong, energetic army vets; in fact, Frank was still an active sergeant in a reserve unit out at Ft. Tilden. He was the best of us; he stood about 5' 10", had a big smile, and had tremendously large hands that could wrap themselves around a construction tool or a .38 caliber service revolver with equal skill.

This particular morning, January 28, we were doing some work for Frank's mother-in-law. She was a native of Cuba who, with her hard-working family, had managed at one point to own all the houses on about one-half of a city block. If you know Brooklyn real estate, you know that was a great accomplishment for an immigrant family.

Her property was behind the old Ex-Lax factory in downtown Brooklyn, and she gave us a lot of work to do. We would start at 6:00 a.m. and work straight through until about 3:00 p.m., when we had to knock off to get to our respective precincts. Frank and Mike worked out of the Sixty-ninth in Canarsie; Frank in a one-man patrol car (a solo car we called it; I still to this day do not know how the NYPD ever approved one-man patrols) and Mike as a plainclothes cop who played decoy while trying to trap a stickup team that was terrorizing Canarsie—very dangerous work.

We spent the day installing toilets and plastering some walls, which was very unpleasant in the freezing temperatures, and then we said our goodbyes and headed off to our real jobs. I drove up to 126th and Broadway, where ESU Truck 2 was garaged adjacent to the Twenty-sixth Precinct.

We knocked off just in time to make roll call for the four-by-twelve shift, arriving at the station house to get a quick shower and get into uniform. That day I barely made it on time.

My shift was fairly routine that evening. Truck 2 covered Upper Manhattan—everything north of Fifty-ninth Street from the East River to the Hudson River. Other units covered more geography, but probably none contained the diversity we encountered. The population in that area ranged from the wealthiest New Yorkers on the Upper East Side's Park, Madison and Fifth avenues to the desperate slums of Central Harlem. It included Central Park, with its tourists, perverts, and joggers; Columbia University; Gracie Mansion, where the mayor lived; Lincoln Center; Central Park West, where many celebrities lived; a yacht basin where some people lived on their boats; Grant's Tomb (actually the U.S. Grant Memorial); and the George Washington Bridge, where people who no longer cared about living would sometimes climb over the barrier on the pedestrian walkway and jump to end their lives.

During the evening, we had a few "assist homicide squads" to search a crime scene, since in those days six or seven people a night were being murdered. One radio run brought us to a person trapped in a vehicle on the West Side Highway, which ran adjacent to the Hudson River from Fifty-seventh Street to the George Washington Bridge. The driver had tried to use an exit ramp in the style of Mario Andretti, and instead of roaring past the checkered flag, he ended up rolling his sporty car several times across the highway and partially into Riverside Park, which also bordered the highway. We needed the trusty Hurst tool to cut him out of the tangled mess of his Mustang.

Gorman and I had resumed patrol around 9:00 p.m. when we heard the citywide dispatcher chime in with a decidedly excited rise in his voice.

It was a call all cops, whether in a rural Wyoming town or the big city, dread: "All units signal 10-13 in the 6-9 Precinct . . . report of a police officer shot. Unconfirmed at this time . . . Ralph Avenue."

Gorman slowed the truck. We both instinctively took a look at traffic all around us. Even though we were miles away in another borough, any ESU truck could be mobilized to go anywhere at any time. Then, before we could even take some comfort in the report being unconfirmed, the dispatcher raised the stakes. "All Units, receiving numerous calls, 911 calls, an officer shot in the 6-9, Ralph Avenue."

Immediately Truck 8, Truck 6, and its partners Adam 6 and Boy 6, the Brooklyn ESU trucks, were on the radio reporting their response to the scene. No doubt they had started in that direction at the first call. Gorman made a U-turn on the highway, as it was better to be facing south, toward those cops in trouble, and he pulled Truck 2 to a stop on the shoulder. Gorman and I sat glued to the radio; we were also monitoring the division radio that included the Sixty-ninth Precinct, trying to piece together the event from radio chatter.

Within a minute, Adam 6 was on the citywide frequency with the bad news. "Central, Adam 6, 6-9 units on the scene confirm officer shot, DOA."

A chill ran through my bones. I looked across to Gorman; he clearly felt the same. A cop was dead, shot, lying in the freezing gutter on fucking Ralph Avenue in fucking Brooklyn.

What happened? We started rolling south. If needed, we could be out there in less than thirty minutes. We wanted to go, but procedure dictated we remain in our patrol area unless ordered out of it, except if we were in hot pursuit.

Now the precinct units were reporting a barricaded suspect at 1234 Avenue K. Dispatch rolled out Truck 8 and other ESU units, including the hostage negotiator. Gorman and I sat. We tried to piece it together. Our first thoughts were that some poor rookie had made a car stop by himself. Next to a domestic dispute, a car stop is the most dangerous action a cop can make.

The more we sat, the more we eavesdropped on the distant action, and the worse I started to feel. We heard the radio calls for the DCPI—the department's press officer—to respond. We heard the police commissioner's driver report, which stated that the boss himself was on the way to the scene. We spotted some live television news trucks heading for the Brooklyn Battery Tunnel. I developed a sickening ache in my stomach. Finally, I asked Gorman to find a pay phone. I don't know what was eating at my insides, but it was bad.

I called the Sixty-ninth's switchboard. Busy, busy, busy. I kept trying for ten agonizing minutes, and I finally heard a voice. "Sixty-ninth Precinct, PO Evans, can I help you?"

I could hear all kinds of noise in the background. It was hard to hear him. I said, "This is Al Sheppard in ESU. Who got shot?" Luckily, he remembered me. I had been assigned to the Sixty-ninth in 1975, when Mayor Abe Beame laid off several hundred cops. So he knew I wasn't a reporter trying to get a scoop on the dead officer's name. Evans, sadness in his voice, said, "Al, I'm sorry, it was Frank Sledge."

I lost my breath. My heart stopped beating. I couldn't believe what I had just heard. Without a reply, I hung up the phone and walked back to the truck in a state of disbelief. Gary knew something was terribly wrong just by looking at the expression on my face. I got into the truck and told Gary it was Frank Sledge. I told Gary to take me back to quarters. I was numb. Just a few hours ago, all of us had been joking together. We had made plans to meet after the shift at our local watering hole, Frank & Edna's bar at Flatbush Avenue and Avenue N. It was a local cop and fireman bar.

I knew this could not be true. I kept telling myself it was a mistake. Back at headquarters, I put in a call to the ESU Headquarters desk. I asked if there was a boss around. Luckily Lieutenant Stanley Carris was on duty, handling the crucial job of coordinating ESU units responding to the shooting scene. I explained that I had to get to Brooklyn ASAP. Carris was a cool customer, a real gentleman, and he knew that Sledge and I were buddies. "No problem, Al," he replied. "Be careful, and call the desk when you get there." Bosses always like to know where their cops are.

I threw my winter civilian jacket over my ESU uniform. I drove my car back to Brooklyn, where just a few hours before, Frank Sledge, Mike Duffy, and I had been installing toilets in Frank's mother-in-law's house. I don't remember the drive, but I know I went pretty fast and did not pay the toll at the tunnel, and in minutes, I pulled up in front of the Sledge home, where Frank, just hours ago, had lived with his wife, Linda, and their young children, Richard and Corrine.

The first thing I saw there was Mike Duffy sitting on the front steps of their house. His head was buried in his large hands as tears streamed down his cheeks. I asked Mike what the fuck had happened. I knew Frank was too sharp and streetwise to put himself in a position to get hurt. He would never let a dirtbag get the upper hand on him.

Mike's face was red and swollen from crying. He had lost a brother, and it showed. He said that what exactly had happened was still sketchy. But it appeared Frank spotted Sal DeSarno driving on Flatlands Avenue. Sal was a local dirtbag parolee, and he was wanted at the time for questioning in connection with an assault and robbery. DeSarno was known as "Crazy Sal."

He was one of those guys who got in trouble in kindergarten and did not stop until he was either dead or locked up for life. His whole family was dangerous; stealing cars was their main source of income, but they were willing to get into anything that would make them an illegal buck.

As Mike continued trying to explain what had happened to the increasing number of relatives and brother cops who were now showing up, I recalled locking up Sal in 1975 for an armed robbery at a local fast food store. It was somewhere around 3:00 a.m. My partner and I were pulling into the parking lot. As Sal was exiting the store, he had a gun in one hand and a wad of cash in the other. I drew my service revolver and took cover behind the door of our patrol car. I shouted, "Freeze, motherfucker!" He looked up. It was apparent that he was strung out on drugs. He never raised the gun. Now I wished he had. I would have put six into his chest. I shouted to him one more time to drop the gun. He complied and lived. I wished now that he hadn't, even though the gun turned out to be a plastic toy. I could not get the thought out of my mind that if I hadn't given him that second chance, or if he had raised the gun, Frank would still have been alive.

Little by little, other cops and Mike put together the story of what had happened. It appeared that Frank pulled DeSarno's car over. As he approached the driver's side, Sal fired two shots at close range, both of which struck Frank in the chest. As Frank started to fall to the ground, he returned fire. A bus driver waiting for the red light saw the whole thing. His report added to the horror. Somehow, Frank's Sam Brown portable radio strap became caught up in the car's bumper.

As DeSarno fled, he ended up dragging Frank's body almost two miles down Flatlands Avenue. The thought of Frank suffering like that nauseated me. DeSarno finally stopped the car when he struck a streetlight at Avenue K and Flatlands. He then ran from the car and dove through the picture window of a home, taking a woman hostage.

Calls to 911 quickly led to him being surrounded by precinct cops and my ESU colleagues. Being the no-balls punk dirtbag that he was, he quickly surrendered. Thankfully, he did not hurt the woman more than scaring her.

At that point, I had heard enough. I could not stand to listen to another second of the horror story. A picture of Frank being dragged down that street formed in my mind, and I haven't been able to shake it to this day. I hugged Mike, and after taking a deep breath, I went in to see Linda and the children. Richard was about five at the time, and little Corrine was just a few months old. They would never know their father—so sad.

Inside, I was greeted first by Detective Lydia Gonzales of the Employee Relations Unit. She said, "You must be Al. I was told you were on your way."

Lydia was assigned to the Sledge family immediately following the shooting. She was there to see to their every need. There are many cops the public never sees who serve in many important ways. Lieutenant Gonzalez was one of those. The next day, Mike Duffy and I were also assigned to be with the family.

I tried talking to Linda. She was obviously distraught and under heavy medication. I held her close. I told her I'd be back first thing in the morning. I went home and made myself a drink. I sat up all night, unable to sleep. It seemed I was in some kind of dream world.

I remembered the time my favorite uncle passed away. My family had just returned to New York from our annual trip to the mountains of Dixie. We were greeted with a telegram. My uncle Grady had passed away while we were driving home. We repacked the car and headed south. I was about ten years old.

My uncle was a big practical joker. All the way to the Appalachian Mountains, I was certain this was his way of making us move back down south. We had discussed this just before we left. But a ten-year-old's method of denial was shattered as soon as I walked into Uncle Grady's house and saw him lying in a coffin, right there in the middle of the living room.

I thought that at any minute he would jump up and tell us with a hearty laugh that he had put one over on us. But this was obviously not going to happen. In the South, the wakes were similar to Irish wakes. There was a ton of food and drink, the nonstop chatter of the mourners, some joking about the deceased, and some recalling of stories of days gone by. It was almost a party atmosphere.

I thought about Uncle Grady all through the night as my family slept in their own beds. Their father and husband, who took ridiculous risks night after night, was still alive.

Like so many of my fellow cops and guys from my West Side neighborhood, I was married young. Daisy and I were wed in 1970, shortly before I entered the academy. I had Vietnam behind me and a great civil service job that would fulfill my desire for adventure and public service and allow me to provide for my family.

On this night, as Al Jr., John, and sweet Kelly slept in their beds, I thought about how lucky I was to have them, and I questioned my own motives about carrying on by always putting my life at risk. Was I being selfish? Were they too good for me? These are questions many cops have asked themselves over and over during the late nights alone that often follow tragic circumstances. Oh, how I wished Frank Sledge was sitting there with me to have that discussion.

But Frank Sledge was not going to jump out of his coffin like Uncle Grady never did. He was dead, and I could not escape thinking that it could have just as easily been me who was killed that night. It could be my family struggling to cope with the loss of their husband and father. Every cop has these thoughts. None of us are far from death. Whether we work at a desk or patrol the darkest, most violent depths of the city, police action takes place unexpectedly, and death is always in the background.

And I, like too many other cops, was by now married to the NYPD. I knew I often put the job ahead of my family. Of course, I took care of my family. I gave them all my money. I paid the rent and I fed them. But I also had my police family, who meant at least as much.

In fact, I spent more time with my partners than I did with my wife and kids. I shared life-and-death situations with E-Men all day, every day. I saw how low a man could sink in his behavior to fellow men. But I never discussed this with my wife and kids. I wanted to protect them from those images and the thoughts that went through my mind. But while I protected them, I was keeping it far inside me and distancing myself, and I knew Frank Sledge was the same way.

I felt despair that Frank would never have the chance to make up lost time with his family, and I vowed to myself that I would immediately begin to bring the Sheppards closer together.

I failed to keep that vow for many years. It cost me a marriage. Daisy and I divorced in 1985. It is a national tragedy that so many police family marriages end in divorce. In 1999, I met my current wife, Trish, and to this day I thank my lucky stars that I am fortunate enough to have mended a lot of fences and that I am surrounded by a loving family that includes grandkids. I wish the same for all my brothers in blue. God bless them and their families, who must survive such obstacles.

But I am lucky enough to have a beautiful and loving family, and I am not complaining.

Around 6:00 a.m. I snapped out of my morass, took a quick shower, shaved, and walked the three blocks to what was now Linda's house. As I walked into the cold morning, the wind stung my face. Today was going to be a real nightmare. I spent most of the next several days at the Sledge home, helping with the children, running errands, and trying to comfort Linda, but that was impossible.

I couldn't bring myself to go to the funeral home. The last time I had been to one was in 1972, when my father had died. I had returned him to his beloved southern mountains. Since then I have paid my respects, but I don't view the bodies. I'd rather remember the deceased as they were in life and not lying in a box with waxy expressions on their faces. And I still could not think of Frank without shivering at the thought of the way he died.

But I did attend the funeral and church service for Frank. As we approached the church, I saw the NYPD Honor Guard of Motorcycle Unit 2, twenty-four strong, all sitting upon their blue and white Harleys.

They were wearing full-face blue wool masks due to the freezing temps. They appeared as ghost riders with smoke rising from the hollows of their woolen masks. Their eyes were not visible as the sun reflected off their mirrored sunglasses.

They would escort the funeral procession to the military cemetery some forty miles east on Long Island. It was going to be a long, cold ride. As we followed Frank's flag-draped coffin into the church, all we could see was a sea of blue stretching for blocks. All were standing at attention. There were hundreds of officers present, and some were from as far away as Georgia and Boston. The service lasted almost one hour.

All that time, the hundreds of officers were waiting outside to honor the family of a fallen brother. As we prepared to leave the church, the sergeant called the masses to "present arms." Hundreds of white dress gloves snapped, as if one, in salute.

Then the silence of the cold January morning was broken by the thumping of helicopter rotors in the distance. In a matter of a minute or so, the NYPD aviation unit was above us. Two blue and white Hueys and two Bell Jet Rangers were flying the missing man formation over the thousands gathered below.

As soon as the last *whoosh* of the helicopter blades faded into the clear blue sky, the silence was broken by a lone piper from the NYPD Emerald Society Pipe Band. As the second note came forth from the drone of the single piper, I knew it was "Amazing Grace."

I could hear the dozens of civilians lining the street on both sides of the church weeping in grief. Old men were placing handkerchiefs to their eyes. I knew the handkerchiefs were not out because of the cold, but because of the sorrow of the sad event. As the last note of "Amazing Grace" floated about the crowd, the bugler played taps.

All this time, our brother officers held their white gloved hands in a final salute to a fallen hero. At the last note of taps, in one brisk snap, all hands came to their sides as they stood at attention. Frank's flag-draped coffin was gently placed into the hearse. We all got in the limos.

The entourage pulled away slowly. The only sound was the twenty-four blue and white Harleys revving their engines. At the front was Sergeant Finbar Divine, the pipe major for the pipe band, followed by the pipers, their pipes folded in their arms. There were no pipes to be played this morning, only the black-covered drums beating a funeral dirge.

The procession slowly made its way to the Sledge home, which was only a few short blocks away, for one final farewell. Neighbors lined the streets with sadness and blank stares etched in their faces. This was a very close community. Everyone here knew each other like residents of a small town, not like in the city. As the procession started to speed up, both sides of the street were lined with the pipe band members, who offered one final salute.

Within forty-five minutes, we were out at the national cemetery on Long Island. I never thought that the motorcycle cops would make it because of the freezing cold, which only made them colder as they rode into the wind. At the cemetery, we were greeted by a military honor guard. Frank had served in the regular army and put many years in with the reserves. Once again, taps was played. The flag that draped the coffin was folded into a crisp triangle by the military honor guard and gently placed in Linda's lap. Then it was time to leave our friend; time for him to sleep for eternity, leaving a son, a daughter, a wife, and a loving family.

"Crazy Sal" DeSarno got twenty-five to life, and ever since that day, I have kept a note on his parole hearing dates. He became eligible for parole in 2000, and before each hearing every two years, Frank's friends and family and friends of cops everywhere write to the New York State Division of Parole to argue that this piece of shit should die in prison. So far it has been a successful campaign. The NYPD Angels Website is filled with tributes to Cecil "Frank" Sledge.

Not long ago, Linda posted these words on it:

> *Not a day or night goes by that I don't think of you and miss you. You are always in our thoughts and prayers. You would be proud of your son and daughter. We love you and you are forever in our hearts. Love Linda, Richard and Corinne.*

And this from Police Officer Jonathan Shekian, Frank's nephew:

> *I was also assigned to the 69th Precinct . . . every day after roll call I would look at my uncle's plaque on the wall . . . I would walk the streets of Canarsie and stop to talk to residents, they all remembered Uncle Frank . . . God Bless You Uncle Frank.*

I felt for many years that if DeSarno was ever released from that hellhole prison, I would do what I had to do. Only until recently did I give up my vengeance, as I began the battle of my life with cancer from exposure to Agent Orange. I was blessed to win this battle—so far. I know that somewhere there is a higher authority, and Sal will get his in the end.

Of course, the world would be much better off today if my friend Cecil Sledge were still alive. Say that scumbag DeSarno did not get the jump on him; imagine if the cop was faster on the draw; maybe he would have killed DeSarno and saved the state a lot of money, as they would not have had to keep his worthless ass in jail all this time.

Chapter Eleven

FIRE, FEAR, DEATH

. . . Grown men lined the sidewalks, crying like babies

The New York City Fire Department is by far the best team of firefighters on the face of the earth. Their job is remarkably difficult. They could, during the same shift, be called on to fight a fire ten stories below the street in a smoke-filled, throat-choking subway tunnel, or thirty stories above the street in the ultramodern kitchen of a movie star's penthouse.

Their brotherhood is not unlike that of the E-Men of the Emergency Service Unit, but of course, they do not carry guns. Their job is always geared toward saving lives; never are they called upon to take a life. That said, despite what the news media likes to portray as fierce rivalries between the two groups that may endanger civilian lives, New York's Finest and New York's Bravest work hand in hand 24/7, 365 days a year to protect and serve New Yorkers.

Many times as an E-Man, my partners and I ran into burning buildings, sometimes before the firefighters arrived, in search of trapped civilians. Practically every night on patrol, especially during the times I spent in the Bronx, I responded to the scene of a fire.

Take Mother's Day of 1974 as an example. I was working a four-by-twelve shift in the Bronx with Ronnie King as my partner. The night had been rather quiet. It was about 11:30 when we parked our truck at the intersection of Fordham Road and Park Avenue. We were across the street from the Fordham University Rose Hill campus, an enclave of green lawns and trees adjacent to the Bronx Botanical Gardens and across the road from the Bronx Zoo. Fordham is a college made famous by the football team of the '30s, which had the Four Blocks of Granite, one of who was Coach Vince Lombardi of the Green Bay Packers.

I was writing up our run sheets. These are ESU reports of the day's activity. Many times, these reports are subpoenaed for court trials years after being filed. Reports could be related to extricating someone from a wreck or a piece of machinery in which case a big lawsuit might be filed between a worker and his company or the manufacturer of the machinery. A run sheet could detail such significant police incidents as a cop-involved shootout. Anything we did during a tour was reflected in our run sheets. As I was working on my last report, which involved an asthmatic child having trouble breathing, we heard a crash.

About thirty feet in front of our truck, a man had jumped out of the fifth-floor window of a tenement. He landed on a parked car, DOA. A shower of glass followed him down. Looking up toward the window he had apparently jumped from, we saw flames and thick black smoke billowing out.

We still hadn't left our seats in the truck. I grabbed the mike and radioed citywide dispatch that we had a fire with a DOA jumper down. "Send FD," I told them, and then Ronnie and I were out of the cab and into the street.

We raced into the building, screaming for people to get out and banging on doors as we took three steps at a time up to the fifth floor, which was the top floor. With some knowledge of the apartment the jumper had come from, we approached the door, and then, as training (again that great ESU training) dictated, we stopped and touched it before breaking through. It was warm, but not very hot, giving us some clue as to the condition inside—fire, but probably not yet on the wall where we were entering.

I stepped back a bit to give myself some room and then kicked the door in. We were met with thick, acrid, black smoke. But we could see that the seat of the fire was in the front room—the room from which the man, now sprawled dead on the roof of the car in the street, had jumped through the window. As training dictated, we dropped onto our stomachs on the floor to start search and rescue. We had no breathing equipment, so we were not going to be able to spend much time in the apartment. We had to move smartly and quickly. We could see across the whole apartment. It was what New Yorkers call a railroad flat. All the rooms linked to each other from the front to the back, kind of like the apartment I had grown up in. Each room even had a window in the middle of the interior wall. This was the kind of apartment prevalent at the turn of the century. They were still found in many buildings and were reminders of the days when recently arrived immigrants were packed like sardines, desperate for any opportunity to breathe fresh air.

When you are entering a fire situation like this, you are placing yourself in a world that has no consideration for human life. Every element you are facing—heat, flames, and smoke—can kill you. You can fall through a hole in the floor you did not know was there, or a refrigerator can fall on you and kill you. These things have happened to cops and firefighters. But you're in there to save someone—an elderly woman, a handicapped person, or a child that may be in distress, unconscious, trapped by the conditions, or perhaps paralyzed with fear.

We did not think about this; we just did it.

We slowly advanced past the first room. The air was getting hotter, and the smoke was becoming thicker as it tried to settle to the floor. Then I saw a man in the corner of the room. He was in a fetal position, and he was scared stiff. I shouted to him, "Get on the floor, stretch out," and I tried to crawl closer.

The heat was now almost unbearable, and I was starting to choke. I reached my arm to him, still trying to get closer. My plan was to drag him out into the hallway. Ronnie was in another part of the apartment, but he heard me and started crawling toward us. Inch by inch, I crawled closer to the victim. I was finally able to get his hand in mine.

We started to crawl back out of the apartment. Then there was this terrifying howling sound. It was as if the fire was screaming at us. We were caught in a flashover. This is when the fire races across the ceiling. We were now trapped. The flames had gone over the top of us, and they now threatened our escape route. We were cut off from Ronnie. Within seconds, decades of paint and plaster came raining down on top of us. The paint was so hot it was liquefied. My back and arms were on fire. I was losing my grip on the man. I could hardly breathe.

To this day, the next thing I remember is being in the hallway as Ronnie was trying to smother the flames on my back. He was tearing off my shirt. I had crawled, pulling the victim about fifteen feet through the hellish smoke and fire, but I do not remember an inch of it. The funny thing is that in 1974, ESU members were required to wear regular NYPD uniforms with the regulation black tie. Well, my tie was not a clip-on. So Ronnie was pulling the tie tight around my neck as he attempted to get my shirt off. He was saving me from the fire while choking me to death.

Thank God Ronnie was somehow able to pull the victim and me to safety. I was admitted to Fordham Hospital, which was just blocks away. I spent a week there recovering from the burns. But the smoke inhalation was a bigger problem. I continued to spit up huge gobs of black phlegm for weeks to come. But I had been lucky. Five civilians, including the poor guy who had to jump from the fifth floor, died in that fire. Ronnie and I got credit for saving many more by waking up the building, and of course for dragging one to safety. I was hurt and sick, but alive, and that was what I was paid to do. Actually, that is what I lived to do.

A few days later, a detective from the Forty-sixth Precinct came to see me. He told me the apartment where Ronnie and I almost died was rented by a black radical group. They were in the process of making Molotov cocktails. These are simply glass bottles filled with gasoline. A rag soaked in gasoline is stuffed into the top to act as a wick. The rag would be lit and the bottle thrown, exploding in a ball of fire on impact. The NYPD lost several police cars to these acts of violence. So here I was, putting my life on the line, trying to save someone I didn't know. And it was someone who—under other circumstances, if given the chance—would have killed me or some other cop just because we wore a blue uniform.

I guess sometimes it's hard to tell the players without their numbers. But don't get me wrong. Had I known that the man I was risking my life to save was a member of a local radical group, I would have gone in after him anyhow. Life is sacred.

And dealing with fire, as any firefighter will tell you, means dealing with instant and unexpected death. After retirement, I myself joined a fire department, driving a ladder truck in Beaufort, North Carolina. I guess I'll never stop needing the action.

But I cannot talk about New York firefighters and E-Men without relating the day Gary Gorman and I were working Truck 6 in Brooklyn South.

Shortly after rolling out of quarters at 4:00 p.m., we headed to Gary's favorite subway station on Kings Highway and Nostrand Avenue. Gary was one of many cops who liked to park near subway stations around rush hour in order to check out the beautiful New York girls going to and from work. I did not object, and I actively took part in the game of rating the girls. One to ten was the scale. You've all played that game. It was a bright, sunny, August day—perfect for our little pastime. We were munching on some McDonald's burgers when the citywide dispatcher said: "All ESU units, Nostrand Avenue, Waldbaum's Supermarket, report of a roof collapse, firemen trapped."

You don't hear many worse calls than that. We were only three blocks away, and before I could put down my burger, Gary hit the light and siren. I told citywide we were responding. "ETA one minute." I could hear every ESU unit in the city reporting its position and ETA. Gary was a great driver, and within ninety seconds, we were on the scene.

We could tell by the movements of the firefighters already there that trouble was in the air. A precinct car directed us to the entrance, and Gary drove the truck right up to it. We were the first ESU or Fire Rescue unit to arrive. The entire building was ablaze—smoke and flames poured out of every opening, but we did not hesitate.

Gary and I started into the entrance. I thought I saw a figure on all fours some thirty feet inside. He was moving toward the daylight of the entrance. Gary and I started toward the figure. It was a firefighter with smoldering gear. We dragged him to the safety of the sidewalk. In a gasping voice broken by hacking coughs, he pleaded: "Guys are trapped, got to get back in, get in there, get some help." They had been on the roof, when suddenly the structure failed, sending several firefighters to the flames and smoke below.

Other units were arriving. An EMS unit with paramedics pulled in. They picked up the fireman and carried him to their ambulance.

These roofs were the common construction for large commercial buildings. From the outside, it appeared to be one solid, arched roof. But in reality, it was nothing but a wooden shell. Lying below were all the utilities that serviced the store. Electrical wires, gas lines, telephone lines—you name it, it was all there; like a spider's web waiting to trap and entangle anything that was close by.

All the wiring and pipes resembled yards of spaghetti sitting ten feet above the aisles, just on top of the hung ceiling tiles, not to mention all the aluminum joists and reinforcing hardware. It wasn't a place you would want to be caught up in any condition, especially a fire.

Gary and I tried to make our way back inside, but we were forced to retreat due to the intense heat and flames, not to mention the black billowing smoke. As we made it back to the sidewalk, we were met with several PD, FD, and EMS units arriving on the scene. I saw Truck 8 and wondered how the hell they got there so fast. But once I saw Tony San Pietro, I knew. He was a rocket pilot. Years later, I would spend many a tour with Tony as my partner in Truck 8. He was there as my partner when I did my last midnight.

Timing was everything right now. I figured that the trapped firefighters had fifteen to twenty minutes of air left in their Scott Packs—those yellow cylinders you see strapped to the backs of firefighters. These are their lifelines. Normally it will supply thirty minutes of air, but under strenuous conditions, it would depend on the individual. We were approached by a fire department lieutenant. He asked if we could breach the wall on the side street. This was where most of the firefighters were last seen when the roof collapsed. The decision was made. We would attempt entry at the side wall. All we would need would be a hole large enough for a rescuer to fit through with a Scott Pack. A three-by-four opening would do it.

The E-Men from Truck 6 and Truck 8 joined us. This would be our job while fire rescue experts tried finding other routes to the trapped men, who were believed to be caught in the pipes and wires in the phony ceiling.

We started our job by scoring the brick wall with our gasoline-powered Carborundum saw—just one part of the remarkable collection of items carried on our trucks. It could cut through anything. Once the scoring was completed, we took to our battering ram, which was normally used to knock hinges off doors in entry situations. The ram is made of steel, four feet in length, and twelve inches in circumference. It is filled with cement, capped at both ends, and has two eighteen-inch handles on each side. Two men could take a steel door down in a minute. Our ram had the words "Here we come" welded on the top. Within four minutes, we had cracked the brick into dust. This exposed a cinder block inner wall. The clock was ticking, but we were confident that we could get in shortly.

Now we were being affected by the heat, which was growing more and more intense. The FD lieutenant ordered a slow, steady stream of water onto us. We had two serious concerns. Number one was collapse of the exterior wall. This would be caused by the expansion of the steel beams as the heat affected them. They would twist like rubber. That would push the exterior wall out without any warning. We all knew in the backs of our minds that we would never be able to escape should the wall let go. We would face almost certain death. There would be hundreds of pounds of brick and steel raining down on us. We all knew the chances when we took this job, especially in the ESU—a place where "danger was no stranger."

Our second problem was the two-ton air condition refrigeration unit sitting on the corner of the building fifteen feet above our heads at the corners of an unstable wall. I recall legendary FD chief Frank Caruthers, who was now in command of the scene, warning through his bullhorn for us to "Pull back, men! Pull back! That AC unit can come down at any moment." He was doing his duty to warn us, and we were doing our duty to ignore him.

By now we knew that there were six firefighters trapped. Their lives were hanging in the balance. Situations like this make a man come to terms with himself. He finds out what he is really made of. It's similar to being in a combat situation. You always hear the macho bullshit of "I'll do this, and I'll do that," but it seems some guys freeze up when the shit hits the fan, causing others to be at risk of serious injury or death. It's like the old phrase "baptism by fire"; once it comes, you will know if you have what it takes. I know of a few persons who were in just that situation. They chose to turn in their badges. It just wasn't for them, especially because they figured they had to do at least twenty years, and they knew that someday the law of averages just might catch up with them.

On that street corner that day, we were all business. We had all the cinder block cleared. I thought that we had lucked out. Normally the block is filled with rebar and cement to reinforce the integrity of the structure. We had breached the wall. But then, to our horror, we were met with our biggest disappointment. Food freezers blocked our entry. And now they were completely filled with water—an immense weight to be moved. We had time for only one more effort. Gary and I looked at each other, somehow knowing what had to be done.

I got back into our truck, backed it up to the wall, and the other guys secured heavy-duty chains around the freezers with our J hooks as far as they could reach, which unfortunately was not that far. We usually used these chains to turn over overturned cars. I dropped the gear shifter into low. I started to move slowly giving it steady gas.

Defeat!

All I could do was burn rubber with the large rear tires. I tried two more times, but the weight of the freezer filled with water was too much. Later on there was a rumor that I had rammed the wall with the ESU truck. That was not true. I had considered doing that, but I thought it would cause more harm than good. But it could have appeared that way from a distance. We were forced to fall back exhausted, wet, and disappointed. But we all knew that we had given our all, down to the last man.

The FD chief called a halt to the rescue operations. This was now a recovery mission. You could feel the agony and defeat of all present.

Within an hour, the fire was deemed under control. Our initial rescue site was now made larger. With the flames subdued, the FD personnel were able to enter the rubble and ruins. In a matter of minutes, it became apparent that our rescue efforts were in vain. All six lost firefighters never made it to the floor of the supermarket. They had been trapped in the utility pipes and wires as I had feared—those tentacles of death that ran above the ceiling of the entire store.

Now we understood that the first firefighter that Gary and I rescued was the only one who made it to the floor. I guess it was his lucky day. But I know it must have been his worst day too, forever having to live with the memory of lost friends.

Grown men lined the sidewalks, crying like babies as one by one, the fallen firefighters were removed from the ashes and rubble. They had fought their last battle. Truck 8 had returned to the scene with brand new body bags and Stokes baskets. Their remains were lifted gently and carried with dignity and respect to waiting ambulances. As each body bag exited the hole into the bright sunlight, all PD, FD, and EMS personnel removed their helmets and caps in a final salute.

As an expression of brotherhood, the FD lieutenant from the company that lost men honored all ESU members. He wrote a letter of commendation to the police commissioner describing the brotherhood and the bravery displayed by the NYPD ESU men on that fateful day.

Chapter Twelve

THE DAY I KILLED A MAN

. . .One side takes lives, and one side saves lives

By March of 1978, I had been a cop for seven years, and almost half that time I had the good fortune of working in the ESU. I was an E-Man through and through, and I had already gained a reputation as a gung-ho guy willing to do whatever was necessary. I had seen many things by this time. I was a veteran of climbing bridges, I was an expert at speeding my truck through crowded streets, and I could drink in the off-duty bars and give and take with my comrades as well as anyone. I was Al Sheppard of "the trucks," and I walked around the city as proud as a rooster walking out of the henhouse.

Nothing scared me; nothing made me hesitate to do my duty. I would risk my life for a mentally troubled civilian who I had never seen before as quickly as I would to protect my partner. Rookie E-Men wanted to ride with Al Sheppard.

But, in my quiet time while driving home to Brooklyn, waiting outside a courtroom to testify, or maybe watching a ball game in Central Park, I began to worry a little about the effect the job was having on me. I realized I was thinking less and less about my grand desire to help people, to sacrifice for the good of others, and to give myself over to those in trouble. I don't mean criminals. I mean the people whose broken bodies we would give first aid: the babies we carried out of burning buildings and the old ladies whose dignity we would protect as we rushed them from their apartments to hospitals.

They were all too soon becoming a blur to me. While I never forgot a person I removed from a bridge, I was becoming hazy on the details. I was forgetting the names of the bodega guys who would give us a warm cup of coffee as we stood across the street from a fire scene. I was hardening in a way that disappointed me.

During the first week of March that year, a week before St. Patrick's Day, I was working ESU 2 in the Twenty-sixth Precinct in Harlem just north of 125th Street, which in those days was considered the center of the worst neighborhood in Manhattan.

Truck 2 E-Men were known as hard guys. Many were former members of the infamous "Stakeout Squad," a unit whose mission was to hide in locations that were prone to be stuck up by armed robbers. They would wait in a back room for the holdup men to enter, and (you would be surprised how many times this happened) they would come out, announce themselves as police, and if the perp had a gun, shotguns would start blasting, and he was likely to hit the floor dead. It was a tactic that worked, and while no innocent man ever died, in New York City, where every shooting is scrutinized, it was a tactic that could not last. These guys were top-level, major-league, professional cops, and I was honored to be among them.

At 3:30 p.m. Gary Gorman and I started our ritual of checking out our truck prior to our tour. We checked all the equipment: the Hurst tool, which was used to cut a person out of a mangled automobile; the trauma kit; and the various rescue equipment on the truck. Last but not least were the heavy weapons. The ESU's main mission is to perform rescue work; our other mission is to provide the NYPD with special weapons and tactics.

As I have mentioned, there is a kinship between cops and the other city worker types who are out there in all kinds of weather, serving the people, and they are always ready to lend a hand to us. Con Ed guys, telephone crews, bus drivers, postal workers, and even the media, which follows our adventures in snow, floods, heat, and smog, all know what I am talking about.

I remember, for example, one sunny March day when Gary Gorman and I were assigned to Boy 2. We patrolled the lower half of ESU 2's area, 110th Street south to Fifty-ninth Street (which is generally considered the geographic center of the city) from the Hudson River on the west to the East River on the east.

We were hardly out of the garage that day when we heard over the radio a report of an injured Con Ed worker at West Fifty-seventh Street and Eleventh Avenue. Technically, it was two blocks south of our official patrol area, but we were available, so who was going to argue technicalities. We knew, because we filed such information away in the patrol guides of our minds, the location was one of Con Ed's massive generator complexes. The building took up the entire city block of West Fifty-seventh Street to West Fifty-eighth Street from Twelfth Avenue to Eleventh Avenue. It was deceptive from the street, appearing to be an ordinary ten-story building. But it had no floors inside. It housed gigantic generators that were responsible for providing electrical power to much of Midtown and upper Manhattan. Someone had seen what appeared to be a man dangling from the slanted roof section of the complex and called 911.

On arrival we were met by several precinct sector cars, including the sergeant. It certainly appeared from the street that this person was in serious trouble. But the only way to confirm this was to get to the roof. It was not as easy as it sounds, because the building had no floors— only two sixty-foot-high generators. The only ways to the roof were the ladders at the end of the building. These ladders rose approximately one hundred feet into the air above the concrete floors. They were bolted to the brick walls. This was going to be a free climb. It was a slow and dangerous process. Furthermore, we didn't know the extent of the injuries of the worker. So this meant we would also have to have our trauma kit available.

We strapped on our Morrisey belts. We mostly used these belts for high-angle rescue operations. The present ESU officers have personal life belts and nylon extenders with large hooks affixed to the ends. The

Morrisey belt was constructed of six inches of thick leather and nylon. There was a large hook attached to a steel ring at the end. This ensured safety by allowing the wearer to hook onto a fixed cable or some other stationary fixture. The belt had saved many an officer's life while fighting with a potential jumper on a bridge or roof.

This belt would allow us to periodically rest on our long climb to the top. In addition, I took up one hundred feet of lifeline. Gary waited at the bottom. This way when I reached the top, I could haul up the trauma kit, and Gary would follow with an additional one-hundred-foot lifeline. It took me approximately ten minutes to make the steep climb. I was sweating beneath my uniform, and my arms were tired and cramped as I climbed onto the catwalk that ran around the top of the building. Once I had opened the roof hatch, I radioed Gary and told him I would assess the situation. He was now on his way up. I made my way onto the roof.

After a short search, I found the "victim." He was startled to see me. He was sitting back while enjoying a hero sandwich and a cold drink, and to my surprise, he was just a worker enjoying a relaxing lunch break. He jumped to his feet, almost falling over backwards. I explained that someone had called to report an injured man on the roof. And it really appeared from the street that the entire roof was on a forty-five-degree angle, so he must have appeared like he was in trouble. We both laughed. I was relieved; he was embarrassed. I radioed Gary with the updated info, as well as the citywide dispatcher, who was probably expecting a call for more equipment. "Cancel all additional units," was the dispatcher's order.

Next was the long climb down. If not for anything else, it was good practice. Just to keep things sharp, ESU members train regularly on the city bridges on Sunday mornings.

Our next call was to a restaurant in Midtown Manhattan—a "mob" location. We were greeted by the owner, whose name I will not mention. But just let me say that unless called to duty, a cop was not allowed in that place. The owner's toddler son had been playing with a sink washer, and it had become lodged on his finger. The finger was swelling, and the child was in extreme pain. This was an easy one. We retrieved the ring cutter and removed the washer in a matter of five minutes, all to the promise of a free soup-to-nuts dinner for us or anyone we wanted to treat. So far that day, we had turned down some beer and now our chance for some excellent Italian food.

But the trip to the restaurant got us thinking about dinner. Our choice was Mc Duffy Bar-B-Q, which was located on Amsterdam Avenue and 130th Street, across from the original Thirtieth Precinct station house. This was the best place anywhere for ribs.

The Mc Duffys were African-Americans of a very light complexion and blue eyes. I had gotten to know them well. The story was that they came from North Carolina just after the depression. The family originated from an Irish man who had favored their great-grandmother. He took her out of the fields and educated her. They told me that if times were different, he would have married her. That's another story for another time, and it's most likely the truth.

Around eight o'clock, halfway into our tour, our ever constant companion, the citywide dispatcher, filled the cab of the truck with an urgent report. The dispatchers instinctively knew when something was real or not. Many 10-13s were unfounded, and while they dutifully sounded the alarm, the voice of the dispatcher was often a clue about what we could expect—go in all the way, or break it off in a few minutes. This call sounded real. "Adam 2, Boy 2, shots fired in the 3-4 Precinct. Officers pinned down. Precinct units request emergency service, 177th Street and Saint Nick."

Gary was driving, so I spoke into the mike. "Boy 2, 10-4, responding to 177th and St. Nicholas." We were already turning onto the West Side Highway for the trip uptown. Adam 2 soon reported in, and a supervisor also told citywide he was responding.

About four minutes later, we pulled up to see three or four cops hunkering down behind the open doors of their radio cars, which were surrounding the building on the corner. Shots had been fired at them; several of the cars had already been hit. A quick flashback to the sporting goods store in Williamsburg shot through my mind. That night an E-Man, Stephen Gilroy, had died going to the aid of his brothers in blue.

A precinct sergeant ran to meet us as we pulled the truck up across the street from the building. While we climbed out, he told us one of his cops was pinned down in the hallway next door to the apartment where the shooter was.

He quickly filled us in. A distraught husband had taken a shot at his wife. He missed, but was threatening her and her mother for a few minutes, holding them hostage. Neighbors called the cops, and the man fired on arriving units. The two women escaped during the confusion, but he was still in the apartment, occasionally firing through the door at the now pinned-down cop in the hallway or sending a shot out the window.

While the sergeant talked, Gary and I donned our heavy vests and armed ourselves with our Ithaca DeerSlayers, which we loaded with double aught buck.

We ran across the street and into the building, where we ran up four flights without stopping. All along the way, we passed cops eager to help but smart enough to let the experts do their job. As we hit the third floor, we were soaked in sweat and panting like race horses at the finish line. We saw a young cop, a Hispanic kid, lying on the floor in the hallway amidst puddles of urine, a sure sign that junkies used the area to shoot up. He was uninjured, but he was pinned down after almost being blown away from shots fired from inside.

Gary and I exchanged glances. We knew what we had to do, and that was keep running, right through the door. It did not prove difficult to kick in, and without slowing down we were inside. No one shot at us.

In front of us lay an apartment with a long hallway and numerous rooms off to the left and right. It was a SWAT team's nightmare. All we knew was that we had an armed individual who had fired shots at his family, other civilians, and responding police officers. We entered the apartment, one of us high and one low. All the time, we were calling out, "Police, throw out your weapons."

The first room was clear. So were the second and the third. Behind us we heard more cops at the door. Adam 2 was here, but they would not enter unless we gave the okay. Then we came to an area where the apartment split into short hallways. I told Gary I'd take the right one, he the left. As Gary entered the living room area, a male stood up, hands in the air. We had our man. Calm came over me, despite my adrenaline, which was still pumping a mile a minute. I was about to lower the Ithaca when, out of the corner of my right eye, I spotted a figure moving—a fourth person in a room that should have only contained three of us. Gary was moving toward the man with his hands in the air, totally exposed. We were in a slow motion movie. I screamed out to Gary, "He's got a gun!" as the perp was leveling his shotgun into a firing position.

Gary had also spotted the second subject. The room exploded in gunfire. In a split second, two shotgun rounds were let loose. Though we were in a seven-by-eight room, I never heard one go off. Gary missed, but my shot hit its mark. I saw a large red flash explode in front of the man. It seemed to be like a water balloon full of red paint exploding, but it moved in a dreamlike way.

As suddenly as it had started, it was over. A man lay dying. I was slipping in his blood as I tried to disarm him as he was attempting to pull out a .38 caliber revolver from his waistband in one last act of defiance.

The man with his hands up turned out to be another hostage. We probably saved his life.

Many cops check into the hospital for trauma treatment after such an incident. I just did not think I needed it. I had just killed a man, but I was in total control of myself. I had acted instinctively as the result of training and experience. Gary was worried about me, but he was also behaving like the ultimate professional he was. The homicide prosecutors from the Manhattan DA's office interviewed me for hours. They wanted to be certain the man was going for his gun. I became the first police officer to be videotaped in a homicide investigation. I went home for three hours of sleep and a few cold beers, and I reported to the Bellevue Morgue at 9:00 a.m. to witness the autopsy.

This scenario is now taught in training sessions. Be aware at all times; never take anything for granted. If I had accepted that the man surrendering was the perpetrator we were hunting, then there is a good chance Gary's family, or my own, would have attended a police funeral. The perp had many guns in the room, including an auto/pump shotgun, several other handguns, and a rifle. He had hundreds of rounds of ammunition. A lot of people could have died if we had let our guard down.

It is a fact that most cops, the overwhelming majority, never even draw a weapon in the line of duty, much less shoot or kill someone. Winning a Medal of Honor for being in a gunfight situation is not something any cop wants to do. Killing another human being is an incomprehensible act. But I never had nightmares over what I had done. I never looked back, except for the countless times I was asked to repeat the details to prosecutors or trainees. It was part of the job and a reminder that E-Men do not always save lives. Sometimes we have to take a life to save another, either our own, a partner's, or a civilian's. That is why society allows us to carry guns.

I recall an old E-Man I had met years ago. He sold vegetables in Bay Ridge, Brooklyn. I was always impressed with his green 1949 Mack truck. It looked like it had just rolled out of the showroom. Every time he'd see an ESU truck, he'd stop. "Hey lads," he would say before telling us how he was assigned to the ESU in 1928—the era of the open ESU truck. He'd always leave with the same remark in reference to the truck: "One side takes lives, and one side saves lives." I never forgot that.

Chapter Thirteen

TRUCK 6 BROOKLYN SOUTH

. . . Busy, but not many gun jobs

In 1977 I was assigned to Truck 6. We were quartered in the Sixty-eighth Precinct, in Bay Ridge, just off the Gowanus Expressway. It was about two miles from the magnificent Verrazano Narrows Bridge—a bridge we trained on to learn to balance on cables and ignore the view that stretched almost to the horizon so we could concentrate on staying alive while we rescued someone who had the opposite thought in mind.

Bay Ridge is a unique area for a neighborhood in the middle of Brooklyn, which would be the fourth largest city in the United States if it was a city and not just a borough of New York City. It is an area that has retained its small-town feeling because of neighborhood restaurants, some of which have been in business for a hundred years, and single- and two-family homes in which many city employees raised their families. It was then and is now predominantly a white village that is Italian in nature, and what minorities do make it there are the upwardly mobile that before long move across the bridge to Staten Island or two bridges over to New Jersey.

Truck 6 covered all of South Brooklyn, its most dominant border being the Hudson River where it joins New York Bay. The area had a reputation as a country club assignment, and I, still being filled with piss and vinegar and looking to save the world, was not happy about being assigned there.

Three years earlier, when I was assigned to Truck 4 in the Bronx, I was needed to fill in on a midnight shift on Truck 6. I remembered arriving at twelve thirty from the Bronx, figuring there was some E-Man on a job eagerly awaiting my help. Well, it took the guy I was assigned to meet thirty minutes to answer the doorbell, and when he did, he was in his pajamas.

It isn't that Truck 6 wasn't a busy assignment. It was very busy, but not with many gun jobs or barricades. Instead it had a lot of rescue-oriented jobs. The core of the unit was comprised of a few old-timers that were as useless as tits on a bull. I don't have to mention their names. They know who they were. These fellows had heavy political connections, and they used them to get soft assignments. Around the gray table, their talk was of pensions and vacations. They didn't recount stories about being active cops because they weren't. They joked with me and jabbed me about someday learning how to get the most off the public tit. It wasn't my kind of crowd. I had great respect for some of the hairbags, as we called old-timers who knocked themselves out to fulfill their duty and earn the public's trust for twenty-five years and who now were looking for cushier spots as they approached their pensions. They were smart. Why get killed because you no longer had the strength to hold onto a cable on the Brooklyn Bridge or the reflexes to gun down a street scumbag before he got you.

But this crowd in Truck 6 had always been useless embarrassments to the other real cops in the unit who were great men. But to avoid embarrassment, they tried to control everyone. Their connections made them ESU members for life, but these were their lives, not mine.

These were exceptions of course, just as in any line of work. For example, Jack Murphy was a legendary E-Man—a credit to his uniform. He was always there to teach the new guys and always first to respond to any assignment. He knew his job and did it extremely well. Jack is gone now, and is sorely missed even in my memories.

During that first tour in Truck 6, I was read the riot act by one of the assholes. He was telling me how I was going to do my job, mainly telling me to play by the fuck-off rules, not to make the regular crew look bad, and not to try for brownie points during the short time I would be there. Little did he know that I don't get intimidated. His bullshit almost led to a fistfight. If it wasn't for Jack Murphy, I would have put that guy's lights out. If he wanted to sit in quarters all day long, that was his business, not mine. I have always marched to the beat of my own drum, and mostly it was a simple tune: an honest day's work for an honest dollar. I felt privileged to be an NYPD officer, and even more so to have the honor to serve as an E-Man.

The sad part about it is that the bosses knew quite well who these nitwits were. What a detriment they were to the young guys newly assigned to the truck, and they never corrected the situation. I was assigned to the ESU basically because I was an active cop. My job was to help people, save lives, and assist my brother officers and not to spend the day kissing ass.

When I was officially assigned to Truck 6, my partner was Gary Gorman. What a cop! He was spit and polish, having been a second lieutenant in the U.S. Army Rangers. Prior to working for the ESU, he had been assigned to Spanish Harlem and the Tactical Patrol Force. He now was the fill-in driver for Chief Robert J. Johnston, then the commanding officer of the Special Operations Division. The ESU was one of the commands under him.

Chief Johnston was a no-nonsense boss. He was tough but fair, in my opinion; hated by some, feared by some, and respected by all. He was a man far ahead of his time. In late 1977, he created the first anti-terrorist team, which was commonly called the A-Team by the NYPD brass. He tapped the fifteen members of the team from various ESU squads. Gary and I were proud to be selected. Everyone on the team was a former Marine or paratrooper. The chief saw the writing on the wall, and he was going to be prepared for it. He wanted to meet it head-on; there was no room for failure on the chief's watch. We did our training at Floyd Bennett Field in Brooklyn. One of our first missions was to do helicopter rappelling. Both Gary and I had done it in the military, so we were the first down the 150-foot rope. I became the first NYPD member to rappel out of a chopper, and I always tried to be as good as Frank Gallagher, the rappel master. I straddled the skid, pushed off, and smoked down the line. As I was disengaging the line, I was summoned to the chief by a wave of the hand. Then the chief said, "Shepp, a beautiful job."

The chief had received two Huey gunships courtesy of the Department of Defense. They were Vietnam-era vintage. They actually had patches were they had taken fire. After my rappel, it was Captain Ray Hanratty's turn. He was a boss's boss—one of the most respected bosses in the entire NYPD.

It was a shame he didn't go further in promotions. But in the NYPD, you have to be political when you're the boss, and Ray told it like it was. Because he was a no-holds-barred person, the house mouse bosses resented Ray. I watched as Captain Hanratty slid out onto the skids of the chopper and made a picture-perfect rappel. And at the time, Ray wasn't a young man. I stood by and watched as Gary prepared to descend. The chief was in conversation with our commanding officer. Then the commanding officer made a stupid mistake. He stated to the chief, "That's a young man's job; you'd never catch me doing that."

Those words burned Johnston's ears. He should have never said that. It would cost him his command. He was transferred the next day. It was true that the commanding officer was getting up there in years. He was a traditional, old-time NYPD boss. He never wore our ball cap; that was like wearing a green beret. It identified you as a member of the elite ESU. No one else was authorized to wear the cap. Our commanding officer wore the traditional white officer's shirt, regulation black tie, and the official eight-pointed hat, and he wore a windbreaker over that. On the back were big yellow letters reading, "C.O. Emergency Service Unit."

Next on the rope was our CO Danny St. John, a poster boy for John Wayne who was mature, in great shape, and the recipient of five Purple Hearts, all won for different incidents in the Pacific Theater during WWII. Now he was wearing the jump suit and the ball cap. Hollywood could not have cast a better leader of men; he was a role model for a SWAT commander.

Well, St. John became the new commanding officer of the ESU. I felt sorry for the ex-commanding officer. But Chief Johnston expected his bosses to do what the regular ESU members did. No exceptions. No excuses. The chief demanded and expected 110 percent for his men 24/7; he would settle for nothing less.

The press called Johnston "Patton," and he took that as a source of pride. The day the Deputy Commissioner for Public Information (DCPI) decided to unveil the new choppers for the media, Johnston piled the reporters and their cameramen onto a small boat in Jamaica Bay so they could get a good look at the Hueys practicing a water rescue.

He joined them on the boat. When the choppers came into the area, they kicked up quite a swell, and one of the more glamorous television reporters got a soaking, and to make matters worse, her cameraman dropped his camera into the boat, which was somewhat filled with water. It was ruined. Chief Johnston was accused by some of the water-logged reporters of planning the whole thing. He just laughed, and before long everyone was laughing. What a guy he was: tough, smart, fair—a model for all of us to follow.

Despite its flaws, Gary and I did well in Truck 6. We wanted to work, and there was plenty of work to do. Take the day in December 1977 when a teenager got himself impaled on some old trolley track.

That winter, as seemed typical for the '70s, we had a tremendous amount of snow. We had spent most of the winter doing extractions of persons trapped in vehicles. In NYC, no one slows down. At about 2:00 p.m. one snowy December day, we were dispatched to New Utrecht Avenue and Avenue J after hearing "report of a person impaled on a trolley track."

We were not that far away, but the weather conditions caused our response time to suffer. We were in the middle of another blizzard. It was hard to keep the windshield clear of the fog and condensation. I hit the light and siren but was careful with the accelerator. I threw the truck into low gear. This would give us additional traction. The ESU trucks were heavy-duty; plowing our way was less difficult than it would have been for other drivers.

As we approached the intersection of the incident, there was a massive crowd in the street despite the blowing snow and temperatures in the single numbers. As I exited our unit, horizontally blowing snow stung my face like a thousand bees. As I made my way through the crowd with our trauma kit in hand, I was able to see what we had. I called back to Gary to bring the oxygen.

This kid was losing a lot of blood. We had to get some oxygen pumping into his body forthwith. I did a quick assessment of the medical condition of the victim. It appeared that this kid was "street skiing," most likely riding the back of a truck or bus for both a cheap thrill and an even cheaper ride.

It's amazing what city kids do for thrills. Timing is everything in life. A snow plow must have preceded his trip by a few minutes, clearing snow from the main traffic lane, but also inadvertently lifting up an old trolley track, leaving it sticking like a spear into the air.

If it hadn't just happened right before this poor kid came along, the back of a truck or a car surely would have hit the protruding, spearlike railroad track, a leftover reminder of the old Brooklyn trolley system. As a matter of fact, the Dodgers, when playing in Brooklyn, got their name because of the people dodging the trolley cars. So the Brooklyn Dodgers were born. The track had been ripped from the cobblestone street, where it had lain dormant for fifty years or more.

I took a closer look at the kid to discover that he had a spear-shaped metal rail protruding from his left shoulder. I couldn't figure out how he got into this unfortunate situation. The track was pulled up approximately two and one-half feet on an angle. It caught him in the left buttock, shot up through his body, and exited at the left shoulder. Every EMT knows that an impaled object is never to be removed unless it is in the cheek or the mouth. Unfortunately, he impaled the wrong cheek.

We had a lot of negative things to deal with here, such as the freezing temperatures and also not knowing if he had suffered any internal injuries. And most of all, how were we going to effect this rescue? He was alert, but in obvious and extreme pain. Gary radioed central: "Have a doctor respond with the EMS crew."

The extreme weather conditions had EMS in a delayed response mode. We had to work fast. We didn't know when EMS would get there. Gary explained this unusual request to central. I can't recall a doctor responding to a call like this before. The weather was getting worse. My hands started to go numb. I'd had several impaling cases in the past, but this was going to be a challenge.

We always had to remove the victim with the object stabilized and transport him to the ER with the object in place. This was because severe bleeding can occur if the object is removed. Now time was critical. I decided to start removing some of the cobblestones about six feet away from the victim. Some of the onlookers offered to help, and they kept the kid talking and as warm as possible. Truck 8 was on the way. We would use the torch to cut the rail in half. We had no alternative. The paramedics arrived. They started to stabilize the victim. *Great*, I thought, *at least they will be pumping IVs into the kid*.

When Truck 8 arrived on the scene, I spoke with Tony San Pietro and explained that we would have to torch the rail. Within two minutes, Tony had snapped the protective goggles on his face and started to burn. Once again, an E-Man had the necessary skills and tools at hand to meet the challenge. Tony's torch burned bright blue at the hottest point of the cutting torch.

Now remember, this is the same as a railroad train track in density. It was going to take some time to accomplish our mission. And time was critical if we were to save this young man's life. Tony was kneeling over the track like a surgeon over a patient in the operating room, slow and steady. After ten minutes, we saw that Tony had cut halfway into the rail. There was still over four inches to go. The entire time, we and the victim were being assaulted by the blinding snow and wind. It seemed that it was getting even colder, which it probably was, as the temperature normally dropped in the late afternoon. In addition, we had to constantly monitor the temperature of the rail, making sure that the rail was not heating up near the area of the victim. Heat travels in metal. It would be a shame to save him from the impalement but lose him to burns.

Our attack continued. We were about three-quarters of the way through the rail. An unmarked NYPD Highway Patrol Unit arrived.

His passenger was a surgeon from Kings County Hospital trauma center. His decision was swift and to the point. We could waste no more time. Still uncertain of internal injuries, we had to break the rules. The kid had to be removed now. EMS had already pumped two bags of fluid into his system. He was now in shock, and his body core temperature was dropping. At the direction of the doctor, Tony, his partner, and Gary stabilized the sides of the victim. I was instructed to stabilize his legs. At the doctor's call, we started to slowly slide the kid off the rail. One slip would cause this kid his life.

After a couple of tense minutes that seemed like forever, he was freed. As the highway patrol car and ambulance sped off into the storm—more civil servants risking their own safety to save that kid—we started to collect our rescue equipment, putting it back on Truck 6. We would have to stop at Kings County ER to get the information for our report. We were all frozen to the bone, and Tony's hands were bleeding.

In the ER, I was shocked to see the kid sitting up in the gurney, a cup of hot chocolate in his hands, while surrounded by his family. Not one of his organs had been touched by the track. He was a lucky, lucky fellow. Other than two wounds, one in the butt and one in the shoulder, he was doing okay. The family thanked us. The doctor credited the ESU with saving the kid's life.

There was a very warm feeling around that gurney. This was why guys like Gary and me and Jack Murphy and Dan St. John did this job. There was great risk and great rewards, not necessarily—actually definitely not—in the paycheck, but I considered myself a lucky human being for having been able to save this kid in this manner. The gratitude of that family and the praise of that doctor were all we needed.

After my hands thawed out, I started the report—there were always the reports—and soon we were back on patrol, waiting for the next assignment.

Chapter Fourteen

THE GORILLA IN THE ELEVATOR

… You know what happens to people who shoot cops

New York's skyline is the most distinctive in the world. Its skyscrapers are the most impressive, if no longer the tallest. Look up "skyscraper" in the dictionary, and chances are there is a picture of the Empire State Building, the most famous building in the world.

E-Men may appreciate the beauty of the skyline and the skyscrapers that make it so special, but E-Men learn to hate the tall buildings and to look at them like they look at not-so-favored relatives; they're okay and necessary, but I wish I never had to visit them.

What the E-Man knows is that inside every friendly skyscraper lay thousands of stairs and at least one evil beast known as the elevator.

Every year, hundreds of elevators break down in New York, and while incidents of them plunging into the basement are extremely rare thanks to their safety technology, it is common that they break down while carrying passengers between floors.

The first to get the call when an elevator is discovered stuck somewhere is the 911 operator, and that means an ESU unit will be on the scene very quickly.

We are told in ESU training and reminded by our on-the-job mentors that all elevator jobs are highly dangerous.

Police officers have been seriously injured trying to extricate trapped passengers from elevators. While I was on the job in 1978, a brother in blue, James O. Washington, was even killed after being hit by one while trying to investigate a vandalized elevator in a housing project in Far Rockaway; may he rest in peace. A kid had misjudged the height of his target when trying to jump into an elevator shaft, and he had apparently broken a leg when he jumped and missed the roof of the car. He was in agony, having been caught between the elevator car and the elevator shaft. The officer opened yet another set of doors on a floor above in a shaft adjacent to the stuck elevator and stuck his head into the dark shaft. He was decapitated when the elevator in that shaft started running. The reckless elevator surfer also died from loss of blood by the time rescuers got to him.

Most freight elevators in Manhattan are large enough to hold an automobile. In fact, there are parking garages that routinely use elevators to move cars from one parking level to another. The skills you learn and the knowledge you gain as an E-Man that most people would not care a damn about are amazing. For instance, I know that most elevators actually swing freely in their shafts. There are series of brackets with large rubber wheels attached to the corners of the elevator cars. These rubber wheels ride on metal tracks that are similar to monorails.

Once these brackets and attached wheels are removed, the car will have from three to twelve inches of play. Of course, it is still suspended by its cables, but the car can then be moved from side to side, which we accomplished by using air jacks, hydraulic jacks, or the Jaws of Life—the indispensable Hurst tool.

I have lost count of all the persons I extricated from wrecked cars, under subway trains, or building collapses. Looking back on my E-Man days, I realize that I had become cold and somewhat indifferent to that part of the job. Once, my partner and I even had to dismantle a freight elevator to remove a burglar who had his leg pinned between the car and the shaft. Our rescue of the thief took almost two hours.

Deep down I cared, but I started looking at the victims—those that survived or those DOA—more as numbers on my job reports than as real people. After a while of being face-to-face with suffering victims in situations in which you can smell their fear and the body fluids they have eliminated during their ordeal, I guess anonymity becomes a protective mechanism. You stop recognizing the subjects as people, and when you have to move a broken arm or place a pressure bandage in a very private area, you can do it with efficiency. Anyway, I was slowly turning into a rescue "machine."

And I was very good at it. I never needed more than six to twelve inches to free a body. It's a long tedious process that is taken one step at a time. You must ensure that the person trapped is not further injured and that the rescuers are not trapped or injured.

There are neither guarantees nor any one set of rules when extricating an individual from an entrapment. Every job is different. There are various rescue methods that apply. But the most important thing is safety for the victim and the rescuers.

There is also a large variety of elevators. The most primitive are the ones with ballast tanks or tanks on the roof that fill with water. The shifting of the weight of the water controls the raising or lowering of the car.

These dinosaurs are found in the older mansions of the city, the four- or five-story townhouses built by the wealthy around the turn of the twentieth century. They usually have a capacity of only two or three persons.

On one particular elevator job, we found ourselves in the Harlem home of Butterfly McQueen. She was the Academy Award–winning actress who portrayed the young house servant in *Gone with the Wind*. She had a beautiful, old brownstone home by Mt. Morris Park. Her elevator was run by a water tank, and when it sprang a leak, she was trapped between floors of her elegant four-story home.

We were able to get into the shaft fairly easily to temporarily plug the leak. We then refilled the tank and lowered her to the living room.

She was overjoyed, and she was so pumped up that she engaged us in a conversation. We talked about her career and her life in Harlem, where she had lived for many years. She was disgusted that drugs had destroyed most of her neighborhood.

We spent about an hour with her, recalling the days gone by during which Harlem was an entertainment mecca for all communities. Finally, after agreeing to a slice of pecan pie, that wonderful woman let us leave to resume patrol. You never know who you will run into on patrol in Manhattan.

Monday mornings were special regarding elevator jobs. It was not uncommon that people arriving for work after a weekend off would find office workers who had been trapped in the elevator all weekend. Usually it was because they worked late on Friday night and the elevator broke down as they were leaving. They were often the only ones there in a thirty-story building, so no one would respond to the emergency bell or hear their calls for help until Monday morning.

Now, depending upon who you were trapped with, it could be a very interesting weekend. Or it could be a very long and boring time. During my career in the ESU, I must have responded to several hundred elevator jobs. Most were routine extrications, such as lowering the car to the next floor and allowing the passengers to get out. Or worse, like having a child or worker mangled in the shaft or pinned in the machinery.

We had several elevator repairmen killed or seriously injured while working in the motor rooms. Once, a poor fellow's arm was pinned under the large steel spool that the elevator cables ride over as the car raises and lowers. The trick to that type of rescue is to be able to raise the cables up off the spool, allowing the victim's arm or leg to be removed in one piece.

We accomplished this by placing 4×4×2 wooden pieces on each side of the victim's limb, under the cables. We slowly released the brake shoe on the spool just enough to raise the cables off the spool and his trapped limb.

Did I think about this kind of stuff when I was a kid in Hell's Kitchen? I had no idea cops did this kind of work, but it fell into that category of helping our fellow citizens, so I was game.

But the most dangerous elevator job I responded to had nothing to do with mechanical failure. It was a miserable, cold, snowy, December afternoon. Around 6:00 p.m. we were dispatched to a Midtown office building. The building was old. It had one elevator car in the lobby and one service car in the rear. *Old* didn't mean it wasn't a skyscraper. This one was fifteen stories high. So it was going to be a long walk to the thirteenth floor, where the stalled car was.

We had to schlep about one hundred pounds of large tools, including a portable generator and a small version of the Hurst tool that was operated by hand. It was small, but very effective for popping doors. It must have weighed about sixty pounds in its metal carrying case. We finally made our way to the floor, soaked in sweat. You don't want to have to make that climb again—at least not with all the tools. It always felt much better on the way down. I knew that the people trapped would just be happy not to spend the entire weekend stuck in a cold, dark elevator car. In the ESU, you do the big jobs as well as the small ones. It's all part of being an NYPD ESU officer.

This could be as easy as using one of the various elevator keys we had in the ESU. There are several types, but they only work on particular models of elevators. It could require that we dismantle the entire door. It depended on whether the car had single or double doors, and a variety of other technical factors. Sometimes it would be necessary to go to the floor above the stuck car and remove the persons on board using the trapdoor. We usually didn't want to do that because it was too dangerous. One reason for this is that every car roof is full of oil, grease, debris, rags, and various hoses and cables that make it a dangerous venture. But there were times we had no choice.

Once we got settled outside the car, I called to the people inside, "We should have you out in a couple of minutes." The response was, "Who are you, the repairman or the super?" I replied, "No, NYPD ESU." I could have sworn I heard "Oh shit," and some muffled voices—a strange way to thank your rescuers.

I began the rescue by using the double drop key. I found it strange that the car was level with the floor. Most of the time, the car is below or above the floor. The braking system trips, and the car stops with a violent jerk. I continued to try and catch the lever to open the door. It had to be done by feel. You couldn't see inside. It took practice. After ten minutes,

I was becoming frustrated. I had done this dozens of times. Now it wouldn't work. We would have to remove the entire outer door. This would cause major damage, and it would be an expensive afternoon for the building's owner. Whenever possible, we tried to do as little damage as possible. We were not the fire department. Their mentality was to tear everything up; whether this was from lack of concern or lack of training I am not sure. That was their MO on all types of extractions, especially when their supper was getting cold and the media was not on the scene to record their exploits.

Next we moved along to the heavy tools: pinch bars and huge crowbars. Every inch we gained had to be secured. This was done by placing wooden chocks between the doors after every movement we made. This would not allow the door to spring back. This could, and most likely would, seriously injure someone. After about twenty minutes of continued sweating, we breached the outer door. Now we could see the problem. The interior door had come off its track. It was mangled like a piece of aluminum foil. Now it was obvious what had happened.

Strangely, as we were working to free the occupants, there was no communication between us. I figured that they were just waiting out the time. When we shined our spotlight into the car, we could see blood on the floor. Then, without any warning, one of the passengers tried to push past us from inside the car.

He shoved his way through the partial opening and bowled me over. As beat as I was, I tried to tackle him. Finally, my partner and I were able to take him down. We didn't know if we had a psycho or what. My first thought was that he just could not stand being cooped up for one more minute. But he kept battling us in the corridor outside the elevator. He was kicking at us and squirming until we got him cuffed. I couldn't see any obvious injuries on him. As we caught our breath, we heard moaning coming from the dark elevator car. A young man was lying on the floor. His left pant leg was torn and soaked in blood. At first I thought that he had been injured when the interior door buckled.

We radioed for a precinct unit to respond as well as NYC EMS paramedics. We knew he had a serious loss of blood. He was incoherent and going in and out of consciousness. Every member of the ESU is a New York State certified EMT, so we were able to control his bleeding and administer oxygen. As usual, it took only a few minutes for NYC EMS to respond. A city of several million people, especially at rush hour on a snowy day, makes for a very busy place.

We still didn't know what the deal was here. As a routine task, we had to record the elevator's last inspection date for our report. So, as we waited for the arrival of EMS and the precinct unit, I went back into the car. Now the picture came into focus. Two shotgun shells lay in the mass of coagulating blood. I called for my partner to give the handcuffed guy a "good toss"—that is, to search him carefully but thoroughly—and to call for the precinct detective squad. The suspect was still muttering to himself, "Fuck you pigs" and other compliments. I guess he was trying to show his gratitude for our having freed him from the elevator. EMS arrived and started pumping IVs into the victim. He started to come around, and although still in obvious pain, he told the story.

He was a payroll delivery man. The other guy, wearing a gorilla mask, followed him into the elevator. Once inside and on the way down, he demanded the payroll sack, which contained about $10,000. When the victim refused to give it up and tried to fight his way out of the elevator, the suspect shot him. The shotgun round went through his leg, and must have hit something like a door lever, causing the interior door to come off the track. I related the story to the detectives when they arrived.

But there is more. The victim further told us that on several occasions, the suspect lowered his shotgun at the door, intending to shoot his way out once we opened it. The victim stated that he told the perp, "You are in enough trouble shooting me. You know what happens to people who shoot cops."

I guess something registered in the idiot's head. He then dropped the shotgun, gorilla mask, and payroll bag down into the shaft. We recovered everything. The perp turned out to be a former employee. It was near Christmastime and he needed cash. Here we were trying to help someone, and he was considering killing us. We were close to death and never knew it. Timing is everything; some are in the right place at the right time, and some are in the wrong place at the wrong time.

Chapter Fifteen

ANYTHING BUT ROUTINE: THE SHAH OF IRAN

. . . I took the offer as an insult

There really was no such thing as a routine shift in the ESU. After all, a regular day for an E-Man could include breathing life into a dying infant, catching a forlorn lover just before she leapt into the East River, or, unfortunately, blowing away a scumbag who just shot a cop.

However, there were times when we performed police tasks that we could not have imagined even with our crazy lives. We called those tasks *special assignments*, and that phrase really challenges the definition of *special*.

For instance, while working in Truck 1, my partner and I were given the job of escorting a convoy that included cop-killing terrorist Joanne Chesimard, the so-called "Soul of the Black Liberation Army," to a hearing. Chesimard, in my opinion was the worst of the worst, having participated in the execution-style death of a New Jersey state trooper and the wounding of another after being stopped on the New Jersey Turnpike.

Given the BLA's deserved reputation for mindless violence, we were well within our rights to expect some kind of brazen attack by her followers in an effort to free her. It was a tense two-hour trip; I kept my shotgun cradled in my lap until we got her behind bars. She eventually did escape from the Edna Mahan Correctional Facility for Women in Hunterdon County, New Jersey with help from some accomplices by taking hostages, and today she hides in plain sight in Cuba under the protection of the pitiful Fidel Castro, who knows a little about terrorism himself. She uses the name Assata Shakur. She is the aunt of the ridiculous and now dead rapper Tupac Shakur.

Another time, we transported a less animate object, but one perhaps more dangerous than Chesimard, from Long Island, again, to Upstate New York. They were nuclear rods, and I will not reveal their destination.

There were other oddball assignments like those—dangerous, yes, but challenging and interesting. The one I remember best was being detached to protect the Shah of Iran during the fall of 1979. The U.S.-supported Shah had recently gone into exile in Egypt after violent protests had taken place against the Iranian government, led in part by Muslim fundamentalists loyal to their subsequent leader, Ayatollah Khomeini, and hostile to the United States, as our citizens in the American embassy were soon to find out.

Although turmoil in Iran was beginning to boil because the radicals wanted the Shah to be returned from exile for punishment, he decided to travel to New York to enter New York Hospital. He was suffering from a form of cancer called non-Hodgkin's lymphoma, which began to grow worse and required immediate and sophisticated treatment.

President Jimmy Carter allowed the Shah to make a brief stopover. The compromise was extremely unpopular with the revolutionary movement, which was against the United States' years of support of the Shah's rule. This resulted in the kidnapping of a number of American diplomats, military personnel, and intelligence officers at the American embassy in Tehran. This event soon became known as the Iran Hostage Crisis, in which the radicals overran our embassy and kept our citizens hostage for 444 days. Once the Shah's course of treatment had finished, the American government, eager to avoid further controversy, pressed him to leave the country, much to the relief of at least one E-Man—me!

Because the U.S. State Department did not officially recognize the Shah's government, the NYPD was responsible for his protection. Our Intelligence Division handled the liaison with State and actually was happy to have us on board because they knew we would do a much better job. Still, I always was convinced the FBI, State Department Security, and perhaps even the U.S. Army and CIA were deeply in the background, watching our every move and making suggestions to our bosses when they thought it necessary. If that is true, I am sure they learned something from us.

There were many times the ESU assisted the NYPD Intelligence Division in providing protection for visiting heads of state, and this wasn't even the first time for me. I was, as an example, also detailed to protect the aforementioned Castro on his NYC visit.

However, the Shah was a different story. We were confined to a double suite on the tenth floor of New York Hospital on York Avenue. Actually, we were locked in with him and his four bodyguards—rough guys who probably served in his secret police force. The suite was located at the end of the hall. Bulletproof glass three inches thick was installed over the double French doors that led to the most comfortable hospital rooms I had ever seen. It was the same thickness as the windows on the limousines used by U.S. presidents.

We wore civilian clothes so as not to alarm the hospital staff when we came and went. And we were armed with heavy weapons and heavy vests. I had a 9mm S&W machine gun with several clips. Gary Gorman had a shotgun and mini automatic rifle. We also had two automatic sidearms. I carried my S&W model 39 9mm and a military issue .45 caliber.

Out of a twelve-hour tour, we spent ten hours in the suites, which was like staying in a luxury home. If attacked, it would most likely become a defensive position on our part, and we were ready for the shootout at the O.K. Corral. Looking back, I realize that I never gave much thought to whether or not Al Sheppard cared to give his life for a dictator like the Shah, but I had signed on to protect and serve, so I never took the time to question my mission.

We were also very much concerned with a handheld rocket attack on our location. This was in the days before rocket propelled grenades

(RPGs) became a fixture in every two-bit terrorist's toolbox, but a mortar attack was not beyond the realm of possibility. It wasn't too long before this time that Cuban freedom fighters tried to launch a mortar attack at the UN when Castro was there. Firing from an island in the East River, the determined amateurs misjudged their range, and the mortars fell short of the target.

Our mission was to deliver the Shah for his cancer treatments and protect him in his suite. The treatment location was located on the other side of the complex, and because New York Hospital covers several city blocks, it was a long trip back and forth. We were receiving unofficial intelligence from the State Department that there would be an attempt on his life. In this day and age, I'm sure the NYPD would have numerous E-Men assigned, but in those "simpler times," there were just four of us inside on two shifts and a truck in the street.

When it was time for a treatment, we would send out a dummy run, using an empty gurney escorted by Iranian security personnel. Filled with pillows, it would appear that a body was covered by sheets in the gurney. This was done prior to our move. We wore long, MD-type lab coats to hide our weapons. The detail consisted of the Shah's personal security (two unarmed persons and two others who remained in the room for location security) and two E-Men armed with special weapons.

We would never take the same route twice in a row. There were times we took the service elevator to the basement, going through what seemed to be miles of utility tunnels and then exiting into the light and fresh air of the climate-controlled hospital. We stood guard outside of the treatment room while his two men were in the room.

Our return trips were sometimes greeted with several visitors waiting to see the ailing Shah. The visitors included Henry Kissinger, Barbara Walters, and former president Richard Nixon. One other constant visitor was a sister of the Shah who lived in Manhattan. She could be a real pain in the ass, bugging him when he wanted to rest and asking everyone a lot of questions. To get rid of her, the bodyguards would shove a wad of cash into her hands and send her on a shopping spree.

Once we were back in the suites, it was lockdown time again. We were treated very well. We ate the same food that the Shah and his men had prepared by the Shah's personal chef. And his food was personally tested by a food tester to ensure there was no poison. Anything we wanted was at our call. We also had a VCR. This was when VCRs were as big as a suitcase. There were dozens of movies to watch to keep us awake.

This was *not* a sleeper job. You might never wake up if the shit hit the fan. Despite all the interaction we had with the dying Shah, we never exchanged any words. One day, about halfway into our assignment, his bodyguards brought us into the room in the suite where he was lying in a hospital bed, and he shook our hands. That was it.

Barbara Walters brought a tremendous pumpkin pie to the Shah on the eve of Thanksgiving. She was the only newsperson to interview him in this country. When she left, one of his men took the pie and dumped it into the trash. I thought, *Shit, my kids would have loved that pie in the morning. What a waste!*

After about three weeks, the doctors apparently decided there was nothing more that could be done for their patient, and it was arranged that he would leave the hospital.

Part of our challenge was avoiding the media. Most of the newspapers and television stations had reporters staked out in front of the hospital during the entire time the Shah was inside. They got stories every day when celebrities came to visit, and a family spokesperson made occasional statements to keep them happy. But the intel guys did not want to advertise that he was leaving.

Don't get me wrong; we always had great respect for the media, and I certainly can't say that any E-Man ever had a problem seeing his mug on the front page or centerfold of a paper like the *New York Daily News* in a photo of him doing something heroic, such as rescuing someone from a fire. After all, just like us, they were working stiffs and had a job to do. But in this instance, since security and privacy were so essential, we were determined to do our duty no matter who was outside, including my writing partner, Jerry Schmetterer, an ace reporter for the *New York Daily News* who I saw staked out in front of the hospital 24/7.

So, under total secrecy, the Shah was taken to a basement garage on a side street behind the hospital, and with an ESU truck leading the way, we sped out to York Avenue. Somehow the *New York Daily News* got wind of the move and had a photographer in a car that was nearly blocking our way.

Usually E-Men and the press in New York got along beautifully, but that photo car represented a real danger to us, so the big truck rammed it aside, and off we went to a place I have promised never to reveal. But I will tell you it was not the same place we took the nuclear rods.

Slamming that *News* car gave me a bit of satisfaction. A few days earlier, a different photographer from another paper had offered me a large amount of cash to get him a picture of the sick Shah. I took the offer as an insult to my profession and ripped the guy a new asshole for even suggesting it.

Chapter Sixteen

THE LAST MIDNIGHT

. . . Numbers on a run sheet

October 13, 1985, was one of those days New Yorkers call Indian summer, although that is not exactly correct. A real Indian summer comes later in the fall or in early winter when Mother Nature blesses us with a few days of unseasonably warm weather.

I was still at Truck 8, headquartered behind the Ninetieth Precinct in Williamsburg, just a short distance from John & Al's Sporting Goods, where I had seen E-Man Stephen Gilroy die and watched the "Rescue Ambulance" come to the aid of those hostages. Thinking back, it seemed like a million years ago, and every time I drove down Broadway past the sporting goods store, I quietly wished to myself that I was living up to the standards set by guys like Gilroy. I hoped I was; I was an active, selfless cop, and I don't think I was kidding myself by believing that.

But over the past year or so, I had been getting down on myself; I was wondering if I had taken too much time away from my family or taken too many risks, and I was wondering, as is a symptom of veteran cops, if I was appreciated at all by the department, by my family, and by the New Yorkers I served.

Brooklyn is a vast place; it is home to more than two million people representing hundreds of countries from Sicily to Senegal. I once heard that Mass is said in twenty-six languages in the Catholic churches alone. Add in the mosques, synagogues, storefront churches, and private homes in which religion is celebrated, and you have the most diverse place on earth.

Brooklyn would be the fourth largest city in America if it was a city, but it is just one of New York City's five boroughs. It was its own city until 1898, when Greater New York was formed. That consolidation took in Manhattan, Brooklyn, Queens, Staten Island, and the Bronx. At the time, each borough was actually a county with its own police and fire departments. Even today each county has its own district attorney and borough president.

Sometimes I felt that each county had its own separate police force. The boroughs operate in extremely diverse ways. To give you just one example, in the 1970s, if you were arrested for possessing a loaded gun in Brooklyn, you got a $100 fine. If this had occurred in Staten Island, you would be looking at serious jail time. These days Brooklyn has a special Gun Court and it is tough on anyone caught with a weapon.

Truck 8 patrolled an area from the Brooklyn Bridge to Kennedy Airport, which is in Queens. It was also the home of Big Bertha. She was one of the NYPD's two bomb and explosive removal vehicles. Her sister was stationed in ESU Truck 2 in Harlem.

These vehicles were tractor trailers. The trailer was constructed of walls made of wire mesh and steel cable that were several inches thick. I had the privilege of driving the unit twice in my career. Once I was carrying a large pipe bomb, and once it was some dynamite. Believe me, a two-hour-long trip through NYC at low speeds with that baggage is no picnic. Every street intersection and every highway entrance would be closed by highway patrol units who raced ahead of Bertha. Our final destination would be the bomb squad's disposal site, which was located at Rodman's Neck in the Bronx.

Truck 8 was also home to the Air Bag Truck. This was a citywide response vehicle that was dispatched whenever a jumper was reported. We had the same type of inflatable air bag used by Hollywood stuntmen.

This special unit was responsible for saving many bent on ending it all. Needless to say, there was never a dull moment in Truck 8, which led the city in armed barricade jobs and in the execution of felony warrants for violent crimes, which always held the possibility of a combat situation.

It was not for lack of action that my attitude seemed to be changing. I was out there constantly, helping people like I always dreamed I could and coming to the aid of my fellow police officers when they were in need. What higher calling is there than that! But I was losing sight of what helping was all about. People were becoming numbers on a run sheet, and my family was practically a distant memory.

My assignment that night on the midnight-to-eight shift was as chauffeur of the actual Truck 8, the big truck, which was kind of "dad" to Adam 8 and Boy 8, the smaller units that patrolled while we sat at quarters waiting for an appropriate call. At Truck 8, we did not wait long.

My partner was Detective Tony San Pietro. Tony had a lead foot; what a driver! He hit the gas pedal and raced for every job. But I guess I'm calling the kettle black. I was also known as a guy who would "fly" to a job. Tony had a special knack of getting through intersections and red lights while barely slowing down. He scared the crap out of me at times, but he never committed the sin of having an accident that caused us to abort our run and call for another unit to take our place in harm's way. Other than Tony's driving like he had a death wish, he was one of the best officers in the division.

Our tour started with the "written rule" of the ESU: Always start with a dutiful inspection of all the rescue equipment on the truck by running every rescue tool, generator, and saw and by checking out the weapons, trauma kit, first-aid supplies, and oxygen resuscitator. You get my drift? Despite my emptiness at this period of time, I never relaxed my dedication to this ritual, which was being repeated all over the city in every ESU truck garage. Who wanted to die when a subway car fell on him because a rescue tool did not perform properly? As I said in the past, the equipment was going to save a life; maybe not on this tour, but sooner rather than later. Being prepared was the most important need we faced.

I was hoping for a slow tour. I knew myself. I was burning out big time. I was weary of the smell of death, the broken and mangled bodies, the burned bodies, and the decomposing bodies. It was all starting to take effect. I always told rookies that "it's not the physical dangers in police work, but the psychological dangers, that will get you."

Now I was hearing my own words in my own head. I had seen too many friends fall into the bottle, divorce, and, even worse, "clean their ears," or as you would say it, kill themselves with their own weapons.

I was already at door number one; my divorce was to be finalized in a couple of weeks. It was apparent to me that I had placed my love of police work over that of my family; this is something I still regret.

After we finished our equipment checks, Tony and I headed upstairs to the gray table—the legendary place in ESU headquarters where everything was discussed and nothing was held back. It was where we broke bread, and on rare occasions, where tempers would flare up. Confrontations between E-Men were rare. But in the ESU, there were many personalities. Everyone was a star in the ESU.

I had just finished pouring a cup of coffee when the citywide radio came alive. How many times had that happened in the past ten years? I left many half-filled coffee cups around the city. We had speakers all over our headquarters, so there was no excuse for missing an assignment.

The female voice, cool and commanding, came over the air: "Truck 8, Adam 8, Boy 8. Reports of a man under, Jamaica and Broadway." By the instinct I had gained after ten years of this service, I knew the call meant someone had jumped or fallen into the path of a subway car. Sometimes a report turned out to be unfounded, but the dispatcher had said *reports*, and that usually meant numerous calls to 911 and a confirmed job.

I thought, *Oh shit!* The tour had just started, and I would have to change uniforms already. How cynical was I getting? Waiting for me was probably what was left of a human of some unclear race or gender. It would probably be just a mass of flesh and rags lying in pieces and still smoldering from the massive shock that had been received.

A jumper was my first ESU job, when I was in Truck 4. It was when the great Jack Shea taught me how to roll a body, twisted around a train's massive wheels, into a body bag. I had a thought that surprised even me as I hit the start button and the big diesel engine roared to life: "I hope this is my last man under job."

Our air pressure quickly rose to right where it should be, at ninety plus. I next hit the buttons that activated the emergency light and siren. Tony, with his hand on the air horn, was clearing the street. We turned out of quarters and headed toward Bushwick Avenue, which was a few blocks away. From here it would be a straight run of only a couple of miles. We would be on scene in about three or four minutes.

Bushwick Avenue is a major two-lane street. It runs from the border of Queens to the end of Brooklyn. As we raced to the job, most of the vehicles in front of us pulled to the side. But this was Brooklyn North, AKA The Killing Fields. Here there was little respect for the police and no respect for an emergency vehicle with lights and sirens on while rushing to an emergency. This was a place where firefighters were pelted with bottles and rocks as they tried to save life and property.

We were making great time. I could see green lights all the way. So far, none of the Brooklyn North "rocket pilots"—the drivers who steered with complete disrespect for all concerned, including police and civilians alike—got in the way. Only one in twenty might have insurance. Mostly they were unlicensed and unregistered. Their plates never matched their cars. These rocket pilots rarely stopped for red lights, and they never yielded the way for an emergency vehicle. Just arriving on the scene of an emergency without having been T-boned was a major accomplishment, as this was the fate of about one precinct radio car a week. But the big truck was pretty intimidating, and on this particular job we did not encounter any resistance.

As we approached the crest of Eastern Parkway and Bushwick Avenue, I could see several precinct units on scene. We would be getting there in a matter of seconds. I parked Truck 8 in the intersection, and as the wail of the siren died down, a young cop called out to me. "All ya need is a shovel and body bag." I hated to hear a young officer talk that way. He had already lost respect for the victim.

This victim had fallen to the street twenty feet below the elevated tracks. It appeared that she had jumped in front of the lead subway car as it barreled into the station in excess of thirty miles per hour. Each subway car weighs approximately ten tons. Several cars had passed over the victim. I could imagine the horror the motorman must have felt as he saw someone jump in front of his train. I grabbed a portable floodlight, which was the first thing Jack Shea had ordered me to do ten years ago in the Bronx, and I walked slowly to the body lying in the street. In the dark, under the elevated train tracks, it looked like nothing more than a pile of rags that might have fallen off a passing junk truck.

But the closer I got, the more I could smell that all-too-familiar stench of burning flesh. Not burned, but burning. Ten minutes ago this had been a living, breathing human being. Now the remains of what was once a person lay dismembered and smoldering on the damp street.

In the past I would wonder, as I approached the scene of such carnage, what could cause someone to end her life like this. How could things ever get that bad? What a waste! These days, however, I wondered more about how soon I could get out of there. I wanted to bag it, tag it, and get back to quarters. This was not the correct attitude for an E-Man; it was no better than that of the young cop who had just advised me to grab a shovel and a body bag.

Now, while standing over the body, I noticed something that brought me back to the moment at hand. It snapped me into the mode that had saved my life, the lives of my partners, and countless souls who needed rescuing in the past.

In the heap in front of me, almost buried in the lumpy mass of clothing, I thought I spotted an infant. *Was she pregnant when she jumped, or is this a newborn coming into life on the dirty streets of Brooklyn?* I thought. I brought the light closer and brushed away some of the smoldering clothing. While digging with my hands into the remains, I was certain I saw a baby. A baby!

I shouted out to Tony to bring the trauma kit forthwith. I was operating on training and instinct. In a flash, Tony, recognizing the urgency in my voice, was standing behind me. This was not a newborn, but a child several months old, wearing a tiny Mets jacket. One of the child's arms was missing. Tony, ever the cool customer, was placing a tourniquet on the little limb. Amazingly, the infant was conscious. There was no bleeding; it appeared that the massive wheels had cauterized the wound.

We worked feverishly to free the child from the tangled mess that was its mother. In a few short minutes, we were able to hand the baby over to EMS, and then we were on the way to the emergency room.

It became apparent as Tony and I prepared to replace our equipment on the truck that I wasn't myself. He asked me what was troubling me. My reply, which just poured out of my heart, surprising Tony and me, was: "I'm tired of being a garbage man for society." There, I had said it. What had been bothering me for months, twisting around in my mind, destroying my sleep, and separating me from my friends and family was finally out.

I was tired of body bags and torn, broken bodies and dead and dying children. I could not even remember, as I wrote out the run sheet whether this child in the Mets jacket was a boy or a girl. I checked the box labeled *M* because of the baseball jacket. It was sexist I guess, but I did not even want to take the time to call the emergency room. It was a far different feeling from the time Jack Shea and I got that kid's arm out of the meat grinder. I visited the boy in the Mets jacket in the hospital for three days.

I was tired of being the guy who had to clean used body bags, washing them with hard brushes and scalding water or taking them to the river and letting the crabs eat the human remains off of them.

Sitting at the gray table as the night passed quietly, I ignored the television, Tony, and the other guys. I was deep in thought, upset with the realization that the stench of the dead and dying had become so embedded in me that I hardly even noticed it. I knew that I had to do something or I would be no better off than being a part of the living dead.

I knew that I had to make a major change in my life, or I would be doomed. Before the tour was over, I made a plan to go to police headquarters at 1 Police Plaza right after my shift ended at 8:00 a.m. I was going to see Monsignor Kowsky. He was the Catholic chaplain and one of the best people I had ever met. His brother was the former chief in charge of Safety Emergency. This was the forerunner of the Special

Operations Division. Chief Kowsky wore the highway patrol uniform, boots included. Highway patrol was one of the units under his command. Monsignor Kowsky, prior to joining the NYPD was a Vietnam combat chaplain who had retired from the service as a colonel. He knew his men well, and he knew his cops even better.

There were several times when the legendary E-Man Paul Ragonese and I took the chaplain to hospital emergency rooms housing cops who had been shot. The three of us were deer hunting buddies. The monsignor and I had become close friends. I knew he would understand. I knew he would help me. I was one of the lucky ones. I knew I was burned out; I knew I had to do something to stay alive.

I came to the police department to help people, and now it seemed that they were just numbers to me—except when it came to the children. Every cop will have the memory of a child who was killed or injured burned into their memory forever. Once you see a murdered, abused, or injured child, it will never leave your mind, especially if you are a father. I never had a problem dealing with adults; I killed one, shot at others, and arrested many who went to prison for long stretches; fuck them, they were criminals who would have killed me or another cop in the blink of an eye. They killed Stephen Gilroy and Cecil Sledge. The grief of the children became my grief, and it stays with me to this day.

I had made my decision. It broke my heart, but I needed a change. I'd have to leave the ESU, the job I considered the best in the entire NYPD. I would have done the job in the ESU for nothing. I know every other member of the ESU would tell you the same thing. I have never seen a more dedicated and unselfish group of people in my life than the members of the ESU.

After a second cup of coffee, I got up from the gray table to stretch a little, and I noticed, for the first time, that my uniform pants were covered with blood and small pieces of flesh.

I was fortunate that the rest of the shift passed quietly. Adam 8 and Boy 8 had some runs, but the big truck had not been needed by the time midnight rolled around. We mostly spent the shift sitting around the gray table and discussing department politics, various rescues, gun jobs—the workaday world of cops. I pretty much clammed up. I just wanted to get out of there.

Then, as soon as I could, I hopped into my old green jeep, fired her up, and hit the BQE, exiting at the Brooklyn Bridge. There was a ramp there that put you smack in front of the underground parking garage at 1 Police Plaza (it has been closed since the attack on the World Trade Center). I walked to the main entrance of the building most active cops would just as soon avoid for the length of their career. It took me a while to get on the elevator. I had several friends on the job, and it seemed that every time I was going to board the elevator, a voice shouted out, "Hey Shep," or "Hey Al." I cut the conversations short in response.

I knew that Monsignor Kowsky didn't hang around 1 Police Plaza very long. He had an unmarked department car. If he wasn't out visiting injured or wounded cops, he was on patrol. I finally made it onto the elevator. I exited the car hastily, looking down and making a left all at once.

Bang, I ran smack into someone.

Not just someone, but none other than Chief of Department Robert J. "Patton" Johnston Jr., the highest-ranking uniformed member of the NYPD. I apologized. "Sorry Chief, I was in a rush." The chief was a strict disciplinarian. Feared by many and liked by few, he expected 110 percent from his men. Nothing less would do. I thought he was a good boss. I had personally seen him help active cops out of jams. We were well acquainted, and he had picked me as one of the original members of the anti-terrorist team, the first in NYC, in 1977. His driver, Reggie Toomey, was also a good friend of mine.

The chief pulled me to the side and asked what was going on. I explained the last shift, my "last midnight." I was burned out and needed a change. I further explained that I was going to see Monsignor Kowsky to see if he could help me get a transfer. I sensed he seemed to be a little disappointed that I didn't go directly to him. He told me he always admired my dedication to the NYPD, and then he asked me where I wanted to go. I was floored! I had never thought of where I wanted to be assigned. The chief was pressed for a news conference at city hall. He told me to go see the monsignor and let him know where I'd like to be assigned.

I was lucky Kowsky was in his office. As usual, I was greeted with a big smile and a hearty handshake. I related last night's shift, explaining that I needed a change. He agreed with me. Then I explained that I had just left the chief out in the hallway. We discussed several assignments. Then the monsignor suggested a unit that dealt with missing and runaway children. It was an investigative, plainclothes unit. It sounded good to me. It was a chance to really help people who needed it. What better than kids! Having three of my own, I knew the dangers that they faced, especially in Manhattan.

The unit worked in Times Square, and this was the era of the Times Square welfare hotels. Literally hundreds of hotel kids were running the streets at all hours of the night. Also, more were pouring into the Big Apple from all across the country on an almost daily basis. The chaplain and I talked for about an hour. He mentioned that he had sensed a change in me in recent months. He thought working in a unit where I could help those who really needed it would be a way to get back to my roots—the reason I joined the NYPD in the first place. I felt much better when I left, and I knew I would be reassigned soon.

I never imagined how soon. I went to work that night at Truck 8, and when I got upstairs, one of my coworkers said, "Hey Al, you're transferred. We tried to call you. It was a telephone message right from the chief of department's office." The message ordered me to report to 12 1/2 West Twelfth Street in Manhattan.

My career now took a dramatic change, and that new assignment became one of my most memorable ever until I joined Major Case Squad. I went on to ten more great years in the NYPD, but nothing could compare to the ESU. I often think back, wondering if I should have stayed. I certainly could have; others had fought off the depression and confusion I was feeling and finished their careers as E-Men. But I have no regrets. Those were great years, and I hope I did my duty well. I am very proud to be a member of that fraternity. Everything in life happens for a reason. I know that no matter what comes my way, I will still die an E-Man.

Chapter Seventeen

9/11

... *We got to get up there*

This memoir has been a project of mine for many years. I have continually added, subtracted, and otherwise adjusted it. My goal was to get some things off my chest, give kudos to those I admire, and in effect shed some light on the ten years that I spent as an E-Man because it was such a special thing to do.

On September 11, 2001, the world changed forever. While every American undoubtedly has powerful emotions tied to what happened that day, E-Men like myself, wherever they served and whatever they called themselves, had an immediate, burning desire to "come to the rescue" and felt a frustration that can hardly be described.

I have stood outside burning buildings where I knew children inside were fighting for breath, I have been at the scenes of air crashes where helpless families died without having the chance to kiss each other goodbye, and I have seen cold-blooded killers escape justice because of loopholes in the otherwise well-meaning judicial system. But watching the events of what we have come to call Nine-Eleven brought my feeling of frustration to an unprecedented height.

The morning of Tuesday, September 11, 2001, was breezy and cool, and the sky was "Carolina Blue" in Beaufort, North Carolina, which was the city I had retired to after leaving the NYPD after twenty-two years of service. The temperature was expected to climb into the high seventies, which was not unusual for the outer banks. It remains warm there far past Thanksgiving Day, and usually until Christmas.

It was going to be a special day for me. I could not imagine how special it would become within a few hours. My oldest son, Al Jr., had just been accepted by the Charleston, South Carolina Fire Department. His start date was October 1. He wouldn't have to attend probie school because he had attended the fire academy in North Carolina a year before. The next day, we were going to celebrate his birthday and his new job. It was good to see he was getting started in a career. He was on his way back to town, and I was expecting him for breakfast at the fire station in Beaufort.

After retiring, I was offered a position with the Beaufort Fire Department. The chief, Jim Lynch, and I had become friends. Jim had been a public safety officer in Durham, North Carolina, a place where the police officers were also firefighters. One day he said to me, "Al, all your experience in the NYPD is going to waste. Come on board. It will be good for you, and you can be a positive influence."

I truly missed the action. Maybe it was because I missed responding to the unknown, or maybe it was the chance for helping people. I had agreed, and as of 9/11, I had been promoted to lieutenant. In addition to that, my younger son, John, was working at Station 54 in Beaufort. We couldn't work the same tour because of obvious reasons. But there were times when the station was shorthanded that we found ourselves back-to-back in a smoke-filled building, attacking a fire. It wasn't a good situation, because I was more concerned with being Dad than keeping my mind on the business at hand. There is no way to explain the feeling of being with one of your sons in a life-threatening situation.

That day, I arrived at Station 54 around 6:30 a.m. The usual smell of freshly brewed coffee was all around our kitchen. It was time for the change of shifts, and it reminded me almost of the ritual of the gray table in the NYPD ESU. The guys were sitting around the kitchen table, shooting the bull.

Lieutenant Andy Di Gavonnie, a native of Long Island, was his usual self, relating the latest training bulletins, telling everyone when he was going to hold the mandatory drill, and reminding us we had better attend. This relaxed, commanding presence came easy for Andy, who was a retired U.S. Navy chief petty officer. Sometimes I jokingly told him, "You're in the South now. They don't care how we did it up North." But it wasn't a joke.

New Yorkers, coming from the rat race of the most competitive city in the world, where the salaries may be the highest (except, ironically, for cops and firefighters and other municipal employees) but the stress of everyday life is the greatest, sometimes have a way of getting under people's skin. We are filled with nervous energy, and it takes a long time to get it out of our systems. I knew that from my personal experience of going south every summer. My cousins harassed me to death, not just because of my rapid speech pattern, but also because I was a Yankee. I never thought of myself as a Yankee, just a displaced Rebel. Rebel had been my dad's nickname on the picket lines. My cousins and I had the same great-great-grandfather, who served in the 36th Virginia Infantry for the CSA. I thought I was as much a Southerner as any of them.

As usual in the firehouse kitchen, no matter if it be in the Deep South or the far North, at breakfast time, the smell of fried eggs, home fries, and cheese grits (well, up North they might not have the grits) was overwhelming. But my favorite scent had taken over. I loved the smell of gravy. It would take me back to years ago, when my aunt Velma would make it on her old wood stove. There is something about traditional Southern cooking. It is most likely not good for the arteries, but it's damn good for the taste buds.

That day most of the overnight shift decided to hang around for breakfast. As usual, the TV was on The Weather Channel. This is the norm when living on the outer banks. We do get some very strong storms, but that's the tradeoff for living in what is, in my opinion, the best place on earth. Somewhere around 8:30 a.m., breakfast was ready.

Our hunger was heightened by the hour spent checking out the apparatus. We had four engines and a rescue truck with a Hurst tool and other rescue equipment. Each had to be completely checked out, just like the big trucks back in the days at ESU quarters.

This meant bringing all the pumpers up to the right pressure and checking all the bypass valves as well as the normal rpm issues. If you are a chauffeur (as they call it in New York) or an engineer (as the guy who drives the rig is called in other departments), it means you are responsible for maintaining the correct water pressure in each of the lines (hoses) taken off the apparatus during a fire. One must remember that there are men on the other end of that line. A drop in pressure means they might get burned or die. To be an engineer is a major responsibility, and it is nerve-wracking after pulling into a street, dropping the line, and getting water to the fire, all within a matter of a few minutes.

On the morning of September 11, 2001, everything was good to go, so we all sat down to breakfast. Captain Larry Fulp was our unofficial chaplain. He said grace at each of our meals. Larry is a super person. He's a top-shelf firefighter and a wonderful family man with a wonderful wife and children. Never was there a mean word or a loud comment from him. I always considered him The Quiet Man. Like The Duke, he didn't have much to say, but he was always ready. There were times I found myself apologizing to Larry. I blew my cool on some occasions, and the words I used were definitely not in his dictionary. I was compelled to just say, "Sorry, Cap!"

I may have been a hotshot NYPD E-Man with a reputation and a chest full of decorations. I killed a man in a gunfight and I saved countless civilians from death or crippling injury. I certainly encountered many situations on the streets of New York that would be unlikely to occur on the streets of Beaufort. But these men were comrades in arms.

I knew from the first moment I met them that I would be deluding myself to think there was something I could teach them about dedication or courage or self-sacrifice. The officers in Beaufort were the equal of those I had met anywhere. Maybe the equipment was not the same, the budgets were smaller, the challenges—well, no skyscrapers or subways here—but the mettle of the men was the same: first-class all the way.

Just as we began to eat, my son John arrived. This was a welcome surprise, as I had both Al and John together. I figured that after breakfast, we could sit down and catch up on lost time. This was, of course, more in the control of the county radio dispatcher than us.

We weren't into our conversation for a minute or two when we noticed The Weather Channel had become the news channel. In fact, every channel was now the news channel. I couldn't believe my eyes. We were watching black smoke billowing out of the tower of the WTC, black as night against the clear blue sky. We were wondering what was happening in NYC, where we had our roots.

The reporter said a commercial jet had just crashed into the World Trade Center. My first comment was, "This can't be. Any pilot would have ditched his plane in the water." The lower bay and the Hudson River were right there; hundreds of square miles of water surrounded Manhattan. Then, within a blink of an eye, another jet struck. At first I thought it was a replay of the first strike. My mind was racing. We all had friends there. Then the reporter stated that a second plane had struck the towers. *This can't be happening*, I thought. *Why would anyone want to kill thousands of innocent civilians?* I knew the death toll was going to be astronomical.

There was a feeling of disbelief as firefighters began filling the room, their eyes glued to the television.

My next thought was to contact my daughter, Kelly. I suspected she was on her way to work. She managed a Wall Street restaurant. That neighborhood was dominated by the twin towers. It was a cramped and dense neighborhood. It would be hard to escape a catastrophe. I called her cell phone. No answer. I tried again. "All lines are busy." I should have known that, but as a father, I had to reach her.

After agonizing minutes, I heard her voice. She had been just about to board the Staten Island Ferry into Manhattan when the first plane struck. I could tell by her voice she was in trauma in between her sobbing and that of the hundreds of people around her at the ferry terminal. I said, "Listen, sweetheart, get on the train and go home. Something terrible is happening. You and Tom load your Jeep and head south."

I don't know if she heard me. All she kept saying over and over was: "Dad, what is happening? I saw the second plane hit the tower. Why is this happening?"

I repeated and pleaded, "Please go back home and pack your car." Finally, she said she was heading home, and the line went dead.

The first thing out of Al Jr.'s mouth was, "Dad, we got to get up there." Prior to moving South, Al had been a stockbroker. He had many friends in the towers. Also, John had many buddies who had recently been appointed to the FDNY and the NYPD. They knew their friends were in harm's way.

My mind raced to the NYPD ESU. They had to already be on scene. These were the guys I had shared a brotherhood with for most of my adult life. There would be guys who trained me, and some who I was able to train. They were good friends—brothers; I knew they would get the job done no matter what it took. But what was the job? Were we being invaded? Were more attacks on the way? Was it rescue or heavy weapons? I was beside myself with anxiety and frustration because I was so far away.

God, why am I so far away at this terrible time? I thought. *I need to get back. I need to be there.*

We watched the towers burn; it seemed like forever. All the while, I was the NYC spokesperson, as Station 54 was becoming the unofficial gathering spot. Several of the town's workers had migrated to the station. I told the guys that there was a virtual city under the WTC: banks, stores, restaurants, you name it. In addition, major train lines terminated at the lower level. I knew there must have been hundreds of people down there. I also told people of the floors I was familiar with, especially the eighty-eighth floor. I was there a few times a week changing the NYPD undercover pagers. I had also been assigned to 6 WTC with an elite federal narcotics unit while assigned to the NYPD Intelligence Division. My mind raced back and forth.

Images of my lifelong friends who were somewhere in that area flashed through my brain. I was worried not just about the cops and firefighters, but about regular people—friends I had met along the way while working in the area. Two of our firefighters, Nick Mayo and Frank

Salter Jr., climbed the fifteen-story town water tower. They unfurled an enormous American flag. If America was under attack, these guys were ready to do their duty.

The station phone rang; it was my daughter Kelly. She took my advice, but she told me that all the bridges leading into and out of the city were locked down.

So I told her to relax, keep up with the news, and get out of there as soon as the bridges were open. I wanted her to come to North Carolina. I thought this might be the beginning of additional attacks, and my greatest fear was biological warfare. No one was prepared for that.

I ended our conversation with "I love you. Please be careful." I didn't want to tell her that her two brothers and I would be there in the morning. If I did that, she would never leave.

Within hours we were driving north, toward the wounded city that was in need of our help. It took about fifteen hours, but we eventually made it to Brooklyn, getting past the bridge checkpoints by showing our badges and saying we were there to help. We decided the best thing we could do was to volunteer to relieve some of the firefighters who had been on duty for more than twenty-four hours. The NYC Fire Department had suffered the greatest losses—losses that would have been unimaginable just one day earlier!

After a warm welcome from the officers and firefighters of Ladder 118 and Engine 205, we sacked out until it was time to go over and relieve the other shift at Ground Zero. One of the firefighters had just brought back Ladder Truck 118 from Manhattan. Because she had been parked on Church Street about two blocks north of Tower 2, she had sustained a considerable amount of damage. But it was nothing compared to what I would observe when we reached Water Street at the base of Tower 2.

The talk around the firehouse was one of hope. We thought that maybe, somehow, there were survivors. I guess none of us could imagine the loss of so many lives, and as someone who had seen a great deal of tragedy, I guess I still maintained a sense of hope, or maybe in this case it was really denial. I was still feeling tired from the long drive, but I was ready to go. I guess it was an adrenaline rush. I had always been able to muster additional strength. The lieutenant came out of the kitchen. "Hey guys," he said, "the NYPD van will be here in a couple of minutes." The level of coordination that the city had put together following the attack was truly incredible. Search-and-rescue teams were established, medical triage units awaited the injured, and NYPD intelligence, the ESU, and feds were on patrol, preparing for another attack.

We got into our bunker gear: me, my son Al Jr., my son John, and Billy Beck, an officer from the Beaufort Fire Department who came with us. Billy had just eaten his first bagel with a "schmear" of cream cheese, and now he was off to see Manhattan for the first time. What a time for a first visit to the Big Apple!

About ten of us loaded into the NYPD van for the short trip over the Brooklyn Bridge and into Manhattan. As we crossed the old lady, I recalled how many times my ESU partners and I had climbed her. As the van came to the base of the bridge, we saw an amazing sight. Ash covered the streets, making it appear as if it was a day after a big snow. Slush was covering the streets. All the trees in City Hall Park had paper in their branches, just like a ticker tape parade had ended. We made our way down Broadway. Destruction was everywhere!

There were major fires still burning in several buildings a couple of blocks from the WTC. Our NYPD van kicked up a dust storm as it circled Battery Park just outside the Staten Island Ferry terminal; this was where Kelly had been heading when the first plane hit.

It was impossible to go west from Broadway. All the streets were covered in debris that ranged from crushed, burned-out vehicles to mountains of rubble. The closest we could get was the corner of the Downtown Athletic Club about three blocks away. The rest of the way would be on foot. Upon exiting the van, our legs were calf deep in ash. Slogging through it kicked up a storm of dust.

I could make out the massive light towers a few hundred yards in front of us that had been set up so rescue work could go on 24/7. Unable to see the "pile" yet, we reached the corner of West Street and Varick. I could not believe my eyes. It was surreal, like a motion picture movie set! *This can't be real*, I thought. I believed I'd turn over and it would all be a bad dream. The entire area, one of the most vital, vigorous commercial sites in the world, was a mass of twisted and burned-out emergency vehicles. My heart ached with thoughts of the men who were working in those units. What had happened to them? What hell had they lived through—or died in?

The pile of debris that was once one of the most important office complexes in the world was approximately eighty feet in height, maybe more including the twisted I-beams and what was left of a major hotel. We hooked up with the crew from Brooklyn. They were exhausted and filthy and did not want to leave. We convinced them it was better for them to get some rest. We told them we would take up the workload for the time being. They would relieve us the next day. They knew they had to get some rest, see their families, and change their clothes. Some had been on the site since the first plane hit.

There were tears in their eyes, and no one was apologizing for crying. The crying, of course, was for their dead and missing brethren and the possible thousands of civilians who might be trapped or dying under the rubble. But they were also tears of anger, a desire to strike back. Many of these men were, like me, combat veterans, who wanted a piece of the scumbags who would plan and carry out this atrocity. But they also knew that right now their job was to save lives, if they could, and comfort the living.

Now it was our turn to climb the pile. We started at the bottom and made our way up to the top. As one cop or firefighter would come down for a break, we would advance. It was the biggest bucket brigade in history. It was a nonstop process of plastic buckets being passed down the line. At the bottom, they were dumped and examined for anything that could be found from airplane parts to body parts. The entire site was a mass of organized confusion.

Needless to say, emotions were running deep. I met fathers digging for sons and sons digging for fathers. We literally saw brothers looking for brothers. Every so often we could make out the sound of special beepers known as PASS devices, which are worn by firefighters, and activated when they are down and motionless. They emanate a chirping sound. At times I could swear I was hearing dozens of them, like so many locusts in a field.

There were several times we would dig into a void after a rescue or cadaver dog indicated that there was a scent of a person. We never found a complete human. I recall only one body bag being passed down the line after a fire department helmet was unearthed. As we slowly passed the body bag down the line, it was apparent it wasn't full. The rest of the week, we just called for large, thick, black garbage bags.

The first night at the scene, Billy found a human hand. It wouldn't be until months later, when all the debris had been removed, that rescuers would find the remains of the police officers and firefighters. All that was left was a gaping hole about one hundred feet deep.

We continued our digging, taking a break every hour or so. There was a headquarters set up across the street—a place where you could lay on the ground or get something to eat and drink. It had gotten so hot on the pile that I chose to remove the interior from my bunker coat. There were massive fires burning beneath the pile. They burned for months. The heat and odors were overwhelming at times. Every time we made an advance into a void, the heat would become more intense. The deeper we went, the worse it became. It was like being a coal miner crawling through all kinds of tight, dark, stinking spaces, only here they were filled with twisted metal and bits of human remains.

While on top of the pile, I had noticed people with lasers on tripods surrounding the area. I figured that on my next break I was going to see what their deal was. I walked over to the guy in front of the financial center. I asked him what the deal was. He was from FEMA. He explained that they were watching the pile to see if it was shifting. If it did, that could endanger the rescuers. One or more of the retaining walls held back the Hudson River, and I had the thought that if the walls failed, all that cold water would hit the fires and hot I-beams. What a steam bath that would create. I knew that if that happened, there would be no hope for any of us on the pile.

We continued digging until daylight. Our relief team was on site. A well-deserved rest awaited us at Engine 205 Ladder 118. The digging had continued all night, 24/7, as it would for months to come. We stayed for six days.

And America would forever become a different place.

DEATH IN THE STREETS

As I was putting the finishing touches on this memoir, my beloved NYPD was struck by two tragedies in a short period of time. First, Police Officer Dillon Stewart was shot to death in a car chase shootout with a criminal who was a suspect in the wounding of another cop. Stewart's bravery was beyond the call, as he continued to drive his RMP in pursuit while the scumbag suspect, fleeing in a stolen car, exchanged gunfire with his partner. Stewart was shot near the heart, in a small area not protected by his vest, yet he continued the pursuit, and the suspect was captured.

At this writing, New York does not have a death penalty. The only thing we can hope for is for the perp, Allan Cameron, to rot in jail for the rest of his worthless life.

The second incident, twelve days later, occurred when Police Officer Daniel Enchautegui was mortally wounded by two thugs.

And then, a horror of horrors, on Christmas Eve, in Jersey City, New Jersey, just across the mighty Hudson River from New York, two emergency service cops died in a freak accident as they were driving away from the scene of a broken highway barrier. They had been called to place flares and help reroute traffic so motorists would not face danger by proceeding.

Our brother E-Men Shawn Carson, forty years old, and Robert Nguyen, thirty, performed their task and then drove away toward a drawbridge that they could not see was open in the heavy fog and rain. They plunged to their deaths.

These incidents, which took the lives of four heroes, are reminders of the unexpected risks that every police officer takes every day. Dillon Stewart's bulletproof vest could not protect him from a freak shot. Police Officer Daniel Enchautegui was off duty and just returning home from his shift when he was attracted by the sound of broken glass at his neighbor's home. He went to check it out and was faced with two stoned-out burglars willing to fire at a cop. He died in the street a few feet from his own home.

Both Dillon and Enchautegui could have avoided death. Dillon could have driven himself to the hospital instead of continuing pursuit. Dan Enchautegui could have waited for precinct cops after he called in the suspicious glass breaking. Or could they have? Probably not; they were cops—true blue.

Carson and Nguyen left a scene where they had just prevented unknowing motorists from driving into a dangerous situation, and they drove into a deadly situation themselves.

When you think about it, you may wonder what brings average guys, our neighbors, our sons, our daughters, and our childhood friends to give themselves so totally to serving their fellow man. I don't know what makes them do it. For me it was an inner need, a calling, or maybe just a simple thirst for adventure. Sadly, I know that as you are reading this, there are probably other names of others who have died in the line of duty that you will be able to add to this memoir. I don't know what makes them do it. I just thank God that they do.

Al Sheppard
September 12, 2007

About the Author

JERRY SCHMETTERER

Jerry Schmetterer is a veteran New York journalist and author. He is currently director of public information for the Kings County (Brooklyn) District Attorney's Office. He has co-authored three previous books: *The King of Clubs* with Jay Bildstein (Barricade Books, 1999), *The Coffey Files* with Detective Sergeant Joseph Coffey (St. Martin's Press, 1991), and *The Godplayer* (Roberta Press, 1978). He can be contacted at *www.newyorkcopwriter.com*.

Al Sheppard and E-Man

Raves from those in the know . . .

A top-notch memoir of an exciting period in the career of a great cop. Al Sheppard tells it like it is!

> - Captain Tom Walker, NYPD, Ret.; Author of *Fort Apache*

Al Sheppard was on the front lines of the most difficult job in police work. E-Men risk their lives every day in many different ways. They are great cops and Al's memoir is right on the mark.

> - Detective Sergeant Joseph Coffey, NYPD Ret.;
> Author of *The Coffey Files*

Sheppard served in the NYPD during the "urban warfare" years and received his "Baptism of Fire" at the Williamsburg Siege. He was a decorated hero of the NYPD and member of the elite Emergency Service Unit (ESU). In his book, E-Man, Al takes the reader on a nonstop roller coaster ride of emotions as he reveals life on the streets through the eyes of a combatant during the turbulent times and the work of the Emergency Service Unit—the same unit that police call when they need help.

> - Detective Lieutenant Vern Gelbreth,
> NYPD-Homicide Commander

Al Sheppard is the REAL DEAL, and E-Man chronicles his years in the NYPD's Emergency Service Unit (ESU) with heart-pounding excitement. Sheppard was on the front lines during the era of Vietnam, Black Power, and the urban drug wars, and he survived it all to tell the tale in a book rich with insider detail and a wry sense of humor. Prepare yourself for a rollicking ride; E-Man is the best New York cop book to come down the pike since The French Connection.

> - T. J. English, Author of *Paddy Whacked* and *The Westies*